Go Gator
and Muddy the
Water

Writings by **ZORA NEALE HURSTON**
from the Federal Writers' Project

Go Gator and Muddy the Water

Edited and with a biographical essay by
PAMELA BORDELON

W. W. Norton & Company
New York ■ London

Copyright © 1999 by Pamela Bordelon

Permission to quote is gratefully acknowledged to:
John D. Corse for interview of Carita Doggett Corse with
Nancy Doggett Williams. The Estate of Zora Neale Hurston for letter
from Hurston to Carita Doggett Corse.
Photographs courtesy of Department of Special Collections,
George A. Smathers Libraries, University of Florida.

The text of this book is composed in ITC Century Book
with the display set in Champion
Composition by ComCom
Manufacturing by the Haddon Craftsmen, Inc.
Book design by BTD/Sabrina Bowers
Illustrations by Christian Clayton

Library of Congress Cataloging-in-Publication Data
Hurston, Zora Neale.
Go gator and muddy the water : writings / by Zora Neale Hurston from
the Federal Writers' Project : edited and with a biographical essay by
Pamela Bordelon.
p. cm.
Includes bibliographical references (p.   ) and index.
ISBN 0-393-04895-8—ISBN 0-393-31813-3 (pbk.)
1. Afro-Americans—Florida—Folklore. 2. Afro-Americans—Florida.
3. Tales—Florida. 4. Federal Writers' Project (Fla.) 5. Hurston. Zora
Neale—Knowledge—Folklore. 6. Hurston, Zora Neale—Knowledge—
Florida. I. Bordelon, Pamela. II. Title.
GR111.A47H84 1999
398.2′089′960730759—dc21   98-28585
CIP

W. W. Norton & Company, Inc., 500 Fifth Avenue, New York, N.Y. 10110
http://www.wwnorton.com

W. W. Norton & Company Ltd., 10 Coptic Street, London WC1A 1PU

1   2   3   4   5   6   7   8   9   0

This book is dedicated to the "sprouting generations"

and, especially, Lauren Claire

Contents

Foreword

This book gathers together for the first time the complete body of Zora Neale Hurston's writings done for the Federal Writers' Project (FWP). Hurston and thousands of other writers, white-collar workers, and "hangers-on" found financial solace during some of the darkest days of the Great Depression working for this highly creative literary unit of the Works Progress Administration (WPA).

Hurston's biography is incomplete without a full reckoning of her FWP background. Her joining the FWP shows her to be a resourceful writer who found yet another institutional means of funding her writing career. Hurston's FWP experience demonstrates the type of treatment that a black federal writer could expect in the Deep South, one that varied remarkably from that of Richard Wright, Margaret Walker, Ralph Ellison, Frank Yerby, and Arna Bontemps, who served on northern FWP units. In Florida, Hurston was given the lowliest position, "relief writer," despite the fact that she was the most published writer on the unit. She bore the added humiliation of seeing less qualified and far less talented white writers given editorial positions at double her relief salary. She watched silently while these state editors passed over much of her work and published less worthy pieces. As in so many other incidents in her life, Hurston bore the hurt silently and kept writing. These submerged writings, now being published as a body for the first time, testify to how great a talent the Florida FWP ignored.

Hurston's tenure as a federal writer enlarges our understanding of her anthropological and literary careers. Her FWP fieldwork and essays link earlier writings. Touched by the wide scope and creativity of the WPA's folklore program, Hurston produced consummate essays and commentary about Florida and folklore, writings that have lain scattered for years in state and national repositories. Several have appeared in journals or were reprinted in part in the Library of America's collection of Hurston's works. The collection published as a body demonstrates Hurston's versatility as a writer, the dynamism of her FWP assignments, and her own interest in adding to the record. When federal sponsorship of the FWP ended abruptly in 1939, its records were distributed among four repositories. The largest number of the FWP-Hurston writings were found in the "Florida Negro" collection in the Florida Historical Society Library (FHSL), and other pieces were sent to the University of Florida Library. Her interview with John Hamilton was found in the Florida folklore file in FWP administrative correspondence in the National Archives in Washington, D.C. The Florida files of the American Guide Collection housed in the Manuscript Division of the Library of Congress revealed others, most notably her WPA presentation "The Fire Dance."

Gathered from these far-flung state and national repositories, arranged topically, and presented with annotations, these FWP writings enlarge our understanding of Hurston's view of Florida, its rich folkloric field, and its varied people.

Hurston's FWP writings show her to be a serious anthropologist whose career had just hit its stride. The massive FWP research engine supplied background material for Hurston's last novel, *Seraph on the Suwanee* (1948), a seminal connection that has never been established. Indeed, the connection between Hurston's FWP experience and *Seraph* is so complete that one can find passages where Hurston lifted sentences from her FWP field notes and placed them in the mouths of her novel's characters.

Hurston's time on the FWP proved satisfying. She met Albert Price III, a twenty-three-year-old WPA recreational worker in Jacksonville, and decided to marry again, despite the twenty-five-year difference in their ages. She was financially stable, as her relief salary was generous enough to cover expenses, enable her to reside comfortably in Eatonville, and help support two nieces who came to live with her. She had all the personal freedom she needed. No one kept strict account of her whereabouts. Her disappearances and often erratic work habits were taken in stride. Her direct superior, Carita Doggett Corse, Florida's FWP director, gave her the leeway that her artistic personality required. With her financial, personal, and artistic needs met, Hurston was able to complete her novel *Moses: Man of the Mountain* (1939) and turn out her 1,500-word weekly FWP assignments.

Going on relief had been an experience that Hurston chose to conceal from family and friends. Only one letter, to close friend and confidant Carl Van Vechten, even alludes to it.[1] Her autobiography, *Dust Tracks on a Road* (1942), written just after she left the project, made no mention of it, nor did contemporary biographical sketches such as those published in *Current Biography* and the *Dictionary of American Biography*. Once she left the FWP in August 1939, Hurston, like so many other federal writers, rarely ever referred to it again.

■ ■ ■

This volume is divided into two parts. Part One is an extended biographical essay that recreates Hurston's life during the 1938–39 period in which she worked as a federal writer. It takes into account the new biographical information that has been unearthed by scholars since Robert Hemenway's ground-breaking but flawed biography, and thus begins the journey of reidentifying Hurston. Only by first reconstructing her FWP experience can the deeper motives and meaning of her FWP writings be deciphered.

Part Two contains Hurston's FWP writings. Many are new discoveries, such as her interview with John Hamilton, known as "Seaboard," who also served as a folkloric source in *Mules and Men* (1935). The collection demonstrates the full range of her folkloric research, her growth as a folklorist, and her continuing commitment to showing the nation the brilliance and beauty of black folk life. These writings extend our knowledge of her anthropological career and literary technique. They demonstrate her vitality and continued commitment to studying various aspects of African American folklore, history, and daily life.

This volume corrects prior mistakes in identifying Hurston's FWP work. An earlier collection of Hurston's folkloric writings, *The Sanctified Church* (1981),[2] lists three essays, "Daddy Mention," "Father Abraham," and "Cures and Beliefs," as Hurston's work when in fact they are the work of other federal writers. Martin Richardson collected the humorous "Daddy Mention" tales, and J. M. Johnson produced the intriguing profile of the well-known faith healer Father Abraham. The original field copy for "Cures and Beliefs" proves Viola Muse wrote the essay, which became a chapter of *The Florida Negro: A Federal Writers' Project Legacy* (1993).[3] Although Hurston was assigned topics in the writing of the state's African American history, none of her writings appear in *The Florida Negro*.

I have arranged Hurston's writings topically. The first section, "Folklore," includes "Proposed Recording Expedition into the Floridas," her masterful essay on the subject that served as a background guide for recordings for the WPA's Joint Committee on Folk Art. It brilliantly highlights the distinctiveness of Florida folklore, a theme Hurston pursues in the second selection, "Go Gator and Muddy the Water." Early drafts of this essay have appeared, but this final version, which includes the "Daddy Mention" tales, has not been published previously. "Other Negro Folklore Influences" was once a part of an early draft of her folklore essay. Following revisions, Hurston decided to make this comparison of Floridian and Bahamian folklore, music, and humor a separate essay. "The Sanctified Church," probably the best known of Hurston's FWP writings, is included in this section as well, for Hurston found in the "song-making," dance expression, and impromptu music of these primitive churches the clearest expression of black cultural life. "New Children's Games," which also is here published for the first time, presents Hurston's brilliant analysis of young people's recreational activities and links them to the wider spectrum of African American culture. A number of Hurston folklore tales, including "Diddy-Wah-Diddy," "Zar," "Beluthahatchee," "Heaven," and "West Hell," are grouped as "Negro Mythical Places," as they were in the FWP's automotive guide to Florida, where they appeared anonymously. Here is some of Hurston's most imaginative folklore: "Diddy-Wah-Diddy," a place of "no work or worry for man or beast"; "Zar," which is "away on the other side of Far"; "Beluthahatchee," "a sea of forgiveness"; "Heaven," where the streets play tunes as passersby walk on them; and "West Hell," where "Big John de Conquer" meets the devil. Paired with

"Negro Mythical Places" is the group "Other Florida Guidebook Folktales," including "Jack and the Beanstalk," "How the Florida Land Turtle Got Its Name," "Uncle Monday," and "Roy Makes a Car." These tales underscore Hurston's assertion that "folklore is still in the making."

The second section, "Florida Images," offers vivid sketches of Southern life in the 1930s. Hurston profiles black life in "Two Towns," including "Eatonville When You Look at It" and "Goldsborough," as well as in her pieces on two enterprises, "Turpentine" and "The Citrus Industry." Her portrayal of her hometown, which originally appeared in the FWP guide to Florida, imparts as few sources can Hurston's feelings about the town that she claimed all of her life as her native village, while "Goldsborough" highlights the fate of an all-black town that did not survive as did Eatonville. "Turpentine" gives the reader an insider's view of one of the South's most infamous trades, while "The Citrus Industry" adds insight to one often perceived to be its most glamorous. The latter is an interview with John Hamilton, reputed to be the fastest orange picker in the county, who describes the business from a picker's point of view.

The third section, "Race," contains "Art and Such" and "The Ocoee Riot," both of which, in very different ways, express Hurston's view of what it meant to be black.

The final section, "Performance Pieces," includes Hurston's last FWP assignments. "The Fire Dance" is the midnight scene from Hurston's Broadway play that she enacted in various places in Florida in 1933 and 1934, and for the FWP in 1939. "The Jacksonville Recordings" transcribes eighteen songs and accompanying commentary from a rare audiotape of Hurston's voice that was made in June 1939 during a WPA recording session in Jacksonville, Florida. With her bodacious insight and helpful commentary, Hurston explains where she first heard these railroad spiking chants, gambling songs, and Bahamian folk tunes. Addressing women, work, and trouble, they enlarge our knowledge of American life in the 1930s.

These readings have been edited only slightly to correct trivial errors in spelling and punctuation and to standardize dialect. Otherwise they appear just as Hurston wrote them.

Acknowledgments

Many hearts, minds, and hands helped in the creation and production of *Go Gator and Muddy the Water*. I wish first to thank Winifred Hurston Clark, who so graciously hosted my visit to her home in Memphis and gave of her time to be interviewed about her bodacious aunt. As the eldest of Zora's nieces and nephews, Mrs. Clark had a great deal of insight and information to offer, most of which has never appeared in print. I wish also to thank the Estate of Zora Neale Hurston and in particular Lois Hurston Gaston, who shoulders responsibility for Zora's publishing, permissions, and affairs. Victoria Sanders, literary agent for the Hurston estate, has extended many courtesies and kindnesses and literally makes Hurston's publishing projects hum.

This book would not have been possible without the early participation of Dr. John Lowe of Louisiana State University. Dr. Lowe offered advice and inspiration, as well as a listening ear to plans to publish Hurston's Federal Writers' Project writings. Without his deep wellspring of knowledge and early guidance, this book would not have been possible.

Numerous archivists and institutions lent support. The Library of Congress staff in the Manuscript Division was helpful in directing inquiries and supplying information. Special thanks goes to Alice Birney at the Library of Congress, who braced herself against the mass of records in the Library of Congress's basement to retrieve *The Fire Dance*, the only known copy of this FWP produced Hurston play. Dr. John Cole at the Center for the Book hosted a groundbreaking presentation, "Remembering the Thirties," that brought together New Deal Arts Projects participants and scholars. It was at this symposium that I met Abbot Ferris, who had been a field writer for the FWP in Mississippi. His remembrances of the 1939 recordings for the WPA filled in critical gaps in the record.

The University of Florida Special Collections Department, headed by James G. Cusick, proved courteous and helpful in research assistance. Joyce Dewsbury, coordinator for photographic prints, helped with the photographs reproduced in this book. Paul Camp and the Special Collections Department at the University of South Florida, which originally housed Hurston's FWP writings, assisted in manifold ways, as did Dr. Nicholas Wynne, head of the Florida Historical Library. A special thanks goes to Andy Simons, inspiration and friend, who was an archivist at the Amistad Center at Tulane University in the early stages of this book. His knowledge of jazz, Hurston, and the Center's resources added to this book. My thanks to Amy Cherry, my editor at Norton, who provided insight and advice that markedly improved the manuscript, and to Ted Johnson for his thoughtful copyediting. Special thanks goes to Dick McDonough, my agent, who "ran front" for the Hurston book.

Special thanks goes to Stetson Kennedy in a category all his own, whose writings, remembrances, dealings with, and insight into the Florida Federal Writers' Project, and knowledge of Hurston shaped and inspired this book. From my association with Mr. Kennedy springs a friendship and association based on our mutual love of and dedication to the 1930s.

Part One

Zora Neale Hurston
A Biographical Essay

I

Zora Neale Hurston has proved herself to be one of the most illusory figures in American letters. She opens her autobiographical *Dust Tracks on a Road* (1942) with the admonition that she is writing it because "you will have to know something about the time and place where I came from, in order that you may interpret the incidents and directions of my life."[1] Yet, despite her bold statement, she purposely distorts her life, veiling her age, early family history, and the "lost years" following her mother's death. Similarly her autobiography reveals nothing about her time on the New Deal's Federal Writers' Project.

In *Dust Tracks*, Hurston wrote, "I was born in a Negro town. I do not mean by that the black back-side of an average town. Eatonville, Florida, is, and was at the time of my birth, a pure Negro town—charter, mayor, council, town marshal and all." In fact, Hurston was born in Alabama, not Florida, in 1891, ten years before she occasionally claimed. Years of guessing have been put to rest with the discovery of the Hurston Bible, the Bible that once belonged to John and Lucy, Zora's parents. The Bible's "Family Record" page documents the family's genealogical background as well as Zora's birth date (January 15, 1891) and birthplace (the tiny hamlet of Notasulga, Alabama, a farming community situated in the shadow of the famous Tuskeegee Institute).[2]

Just why Hurston hid her Alabama roots can only be guessed at. Her moving from Alabama before the age of two meant that she had little conscious knowledge of the place. Being identified with the all-black town of Eatonville, Florida, rather than with the sharecropping and tenant-farming plains of rural Alabama was more in keeping with the image of herself that she was trying to create.

In the 1890s, this Alabama hinterland was a poor place. John Hurston and Lula (Lucy) Potts, who had been born in the area in 1861 and 1865 respectively, married there in February 1882. Their first child, Robert Hezekiah, arrived in November of the same year. Three more sons—Isaac, who died while still a small child (sometime before 1889), John Cornelius, and Richard—as well as a daughter, Sarah (1889), followed. John and Lucy wanted more for their growing family than the sharecropping, degradation, and (as Hurston would say) "soul stomping" that Alabama, with its tenant system, offered. Sometime after Zora's birth and before the arrival of her brother Joel, the family moved to the citrus belt of central Florida.

The family's migration was a critical decision for the future writer Zora Neale Hurston. What would have happened if her family had remained in the Alabama countryside? Nate Shaw, a lifelong resident of the Notasulga area who sharecropped and tenant-farmed, raised his children, and moved as high up the economic ladder as one in his position could venture, testifies to the type of life the area offered blacks: "Conditions has been outrageous every way that you can think against the colored race of people. Didn't allow em to do this, didn't allow em to do that, didn't allow em to do the other. . . . the white man held the final rule over the Negro." As Shaw relates, in Alabama blacks were "scared to run their business together, buy their fertilize together, sell their cotton together. . . ."[3] Blacks locked into the vicious sharecropping and tenant system were totally dependent on the whites who ran the banks and mercantile stores that furnished their farming credit and supplies. The white power structure controlled the economic and educational systems, keys to the Hurston family's later success. Most black children in Alabama who were kept laboring in the cotton fields had little chance of receiving a good education. To send them to school would have denied white farm owners exploitation of a valuable source of labor. The little education provided black children was hopelessly inadequate.[4]

Looking for better conditions and educational opportunity for his children, John Hurston left Alabama and sought a place where in the words of John Buddy in Zora's first novel, *Jonah's Gourd Vine*, "uh man can be soupin' . . . without folks tramplin' all over yuh."[5] John Hurston had heard of the railroad boom farther south in Florida where Henry Plant was building the Atlantic Coast Line down the east coast of the peninsula. Here there was work, good pay, and no more back-bending over rows of cotton; no more fear of the fury of Reconstruction.[6]

In the citrus-growing belt of central Florida, John Hurston found opportunity, and sympathetic whites who donated land for the all-black town of Eatonville, named after one of its white benefactors. He decided to settle there. With his quick mind and oratorical skills, he found a position preaching soon after he arrived. He was pastor of the Zion Hope Baptist Church in Sanford, Florida, as early as 1892, a position he held for decades. With a toehold established, Hurston wrote in *Dust Tracks*, "Relatives and friends were sent for." Dates in the Hurston Bible, an article in the *Sanford Herald* indicating Reverend Hurston began pastoring his Florida church in 1892, and Hurston's comments in *Jonah's Gourd Vine* indicate that the family moved to Eatonville in 1892.[7]

Supported by a growing church membership in central Florida's newly emerging citrus-and-vegetable-growing region, John Hurston prospered. He bought land in Eatonville and built a substantial two-story, eight-room house and a barn. A five-acre garden, a citrus grove, chickens, and home-cured meat supplied bountiful food. Four more children—all sons—were born. Although Hurston very often painted a childhood of poverty and deprivation (especially to white patrons), she was raised with the trappings of a substantial middle-class life and the prestige of being the minister's daughter. The minister then (as now) was ordinarily the most distinguished member of the black community. And John Hurston was no exception. His leadership was felt in the area as he urged black parents to keep their children from working and allow them to get an education.[8] He took an administrative role in town affairs, serving as its mayor from 1912 to 1916. All of the Hurston children were educated. Robert Hezekiah, Hurston's eldest brother, graduated from Meharry Medical College in Nashville as a physician. Ben earned a pharmaceutical degree at the same institution. Joel became a high school principal, and John Cornelius put his education to good use in his Jacksonville meat market. Everett, the youngest, became a postman in New York.[9]

Hurston's mother supported the ambitions of her children as well. Zora claimed that Lula (Lucy) Potts Hurston exerted the strongest influence over her. Yet, little is known about her. Everything we do know about her comes from *Dust Tracks*, where Hurston frames her warmest memories of her mother. Her mother supported rather than diminished her ebullient and often impudent spirit. She encouraged the young Zora and all of her other children to "jump at de sun." As Hurston explained, "We might not land on the sun, but at least we would get off the ground." Zora portrayed her mother as a gifted and intelligent woman who shared John Hurston's belief in education. Wanting more education for her children than the Jim Crow South had to offer, she supplemented their schooling with home lessons. "You had to keep on going over things until you did know," Hurston asserted. Her caring yet exacting mother imbued her with a fierce desire to get ahead, with hope for a far different life from that granted most Southern black children caught in the vortex of farm tenancy and exploitation. Her mother's spirit never left her.[10]

Lucy Hurston's unfortunate death on September 19, 1904, when young Zora was only thirteen, interrupted what had been until that time a warm and happy childhood. In *Dust Tracks*, Hurston claimed to be nine years old, not the nearly grown child she was. Just after her fourteenth birthday, Hurston's father married Mattie Moge, a woman half his age, who was but six years Zora's senior and three years younger than his eldest son. His remarriage to a much younger woman so soon after Lucy's death was destined to cause problems.[11]

Twenty-year-old Mattie Moge could not replace young Zora's mother. Hurston hated her stepmother and expresses her disdain in some of her most vehement language. They fought violently when Mattie tried to discipline her for her "sassy" and "impudent" ways: "I wanted her blood, and plenty of it. That is the way I went into the fight, and that is the way I fought it." A photograph of Mattie reveals her to be a slight, petite woman who would have been easily overcome by an enraged girl who was larger and stronger than she. Hurston describes how she beat her stepmother to the floor and then "began to scream with rage. I had not beaten more than two years out of her yet. I made up my mind to stomp her, but at last Papa came to, and pulled me away." For obvious reasons, after the fight young Zora was removed from the house.[12]

The years following her mother's death in 1904 and Hurston's enrollment in Baltimore at Morgan Academy in 1917, which set her life on a wandering course, have remained undocumented. We have scant information on how her relations with her father and siblings proceeded, why she was unable to complete her high school education, and how her character developed. Was she really a "slave ship in shoes," as she claimed? Hurston tells us almost nothing of these years, only of her misery, her father's abandonment, and her poverty.[13]

Deeper investigation provides some clues to the Hurston family history during this time. Although one cannot say for sure, more than likely Zora was sent to boarding school in Jacksonville. Her vivid memories of boarding school in Jacksonville recorded in *Dust Tracks* make this more than likely. The rest of the Hurston children lived with their stepmother and father. Census records for 1910 indicate that six years after Lucy Hurston's death, the three youngest Hurston children were living in the household of their father and stepmother Mattie. The fact that she is listed as his wife proves that John Hurston did not divorce her.[14] It hardly seems likely that John Hurston, an upstanding pastor in the community, would abandon his daughter. Zora most likely *felt* deserted when she was removed from her home and sent away. Her father's career did not decline after Lucy Hurston's death as Zora claimed. Indeed, John Hurston's best years were before him; he was elected to the Baptist Convention, and he became mayor of Eatonville in 1912 and served until 1916. Sometime after 1916, John and Mattie Hurston moved to Memphis, for unknown reasons. In May 1918, the Reverend Hurston died in an unfortunate car-train collision. Such accidents were not infrequent in the early days of the automobile, when railroad crossings were often unsafe.[15]

Once her two eldest brothers married, Zora lived for a time with each of them. A 1912 photograph shows Zora standing with her physician brother, Dr. Robert Hurston, his wife, Wilhelmina, and their infant son, Robert Jr., proving that she was with the family long before she admits in *Dust Tracks*. Solid evidence in the form of a Bethel Baptist Church register shows Zora in 1914 living with her brother John and his wife, Blanche; she maintained close relations with this couple for most of her life. Elder members of the congregation claim that she was attending school.[16] *Dust Tracks* places her back in Memphis in 1916, caring for Bob's three children.

Bob Hurston was nearly ten years older than his sister, and he may have felt responsibility toward her in the years following their mother's death. No doubt he knew that she was having a hard time and wanted to help her. A family photograph shows Hurston with Bob Hurston's three eldest children. This evidence supports her assertion in *Dust Tracks* that she lived with the family for a while. In her autobiography, Hurston admits her excitement at her brother's invitation: "I was going to have a home again. I was going to school. I was going to be with my brother. He had remembered me at last. My five haunted years were over." She goes on: "I shall never forget the exaltation of my hurried packing. When I got on the train, I waved goodbye—not to anybody in particular, but to the town, to loneliness, to defeat and frustration, to shabby living, to sterile houses and numbed pangs, to the kind of people I had no wish to know; to an era. I waved it goodbye and sank back into the cushions of the seat."[17]

Memphis at this time was attracting droves of rural black Southerners who were looking for economic opportunity. Some settled there; for others, it proved a way station, the gateway north. Richard Wright passed through the city during the 1920s on his way to Chicago and later New York.[18] To Hurston as well, Memphis was a halfway house that freed her from her insular rural environment and provided her a way out of the South.

Dr. Hurston lived in the Scott Street area of the city. He had a substantial two-story home and an office not far away. He was well known in the tight-knit community, a place where "everyone knew everyone." Here newly arrived rural migrants sought to replicate the communal atmosphere they had left behind. In her brief residence, Hurston was sheltered and protected by this Scott Street community as well as by a strong and loving brother.[19]

In *Dust Tracks*, Hurston speaks of her life in her brother's home. She resented rising early and lighting the fires. She chafed under the heavy workload with no pay. But her deepest dissatisfaction was something else: "There was to be no school for me right away. I was needed around the house."[20]

Bob Hurston's daughter Winifred provides a profile of her father that offers additional insight into why Hurston left. Bob Hurston was a hardworking physician who went out of his way to help others in need. He offered his medical services regardless of his patients' ability to pay. "If people said they were sick, he was there," Winifred recalled. He was a compassionate man who made house calls late into the night, bailed men out of prison, and gave them jobs driving him to patients' homes or doing odd jobs around his home. When he died in 1935, many of his patients owed him money.

Kind as he was, Bob Hurston was a strict disciplinarian. An incident from Winifred's early childhood illustrates this. One night after returning home late from seeing a patient, Bob Hurston noticed that Winifred had failed to wash the pots after dinner and had put them on the back porch to soak. Rather than let his daughter's work slide, he got Winifred out of bed and, she recalled, "made me wash those pots. He only had to do it once. I didn't want to wash those pots, but I did from then on."[21]

Given Bob Hurston's exacting standards, there is little doubt that the fun-loving Zora, a young woman of twenty-five, chafed under his rule. Here her account of her life in *Dust Tracks* rings true. Rather than serve, she fled, finding amusement and release by joining a Gilbert and Sullivan company as personal maid to one of the actresses. After her travels with the troupe, she landed in Baltimore, Maryland, where her sister Sarah lived.[22]

In Baltimore, Hurston attended Morgan Academy and graduated with a high school degree. She was now a young woman of twenty-six. Just why she had not completed high school sooner is not clear, but her desire to get an education never left her.[23]

Following her graduation from Morgan Academy, Hurston went

on to Howard University, a place and time in her life she describes warmly in her autobiography. There her intelligence and literary talent quickly emerged. She won second place in an *Opportunity* magazine writing contest and the attention of Charles S. Johnson, editor of the magazine. He encouraged her to come to New York, where the Harlem Renaissance was in full swing, the "New Negro" was in vogue, and white patronage of black artists, writers, and actors flowed freely.[24] This proved a wise decision. Judges of the *Opportunity* contest, influential whites and patrons of the arts, assisted her. Annie Nathan Meyer, who was a trustee of the college, found her a scholarship to Barnard College of Columbia University, and Fannie Hurst gave her employment as her secretary, despite her poor typing skills. At Barnard, Hurston came under the influence of Franz Boas, Melville Herskovits, and Ruth Benedict, towering figures in the new field of anthropology. Together these intellectual pioneers charted the new direction that the discipline would take. Although Benedict and Herskovits influenced Hurston profoundly, it was Boas who molded and directed her career. It was "Papa Franz," as Hurston teasingly called Boas, who grounded her in the field experience needed to launch her career as an anthropologist and writer.[25] He imbued Hurston with his ideas about cultural relativism, a theory that lifted anthropology from the racial constraints of nineteenth-century evolution theory and placed equal value on all cultures. Boas's tutelage sparked in her the desire to switch from English to anthropology in order to illuminate the beauty and vibrancy of African American life.[26]

Boas recognized Hurston's gifts and her potential as a collector of black folklore in the South, where she would have obvious advantages over white researchers. He guided her early field efforts, obtained a research fellowship for her, and directed her earliest field collecting. Thanks to Boas's exacting standards, rigorous training, and stern discipline, early field disappointments led later to startling success.

Once Hurston graduated from Barnard in 1927, she found the generous backing of a patron who would sponsor nearly four years of nonstop folklore collecting throughout the South between 1928 and 1932. Mrs. Charlotte Osgood Mason sponsored not only Hurston but also the poet Langston Hughes. It was Hughes, her close friend and fellow

Harlemite, who introduced Hurston to Mrs. Mason, who was already sponsoring a number of other gifted black writers, musicians, and intellectuals involved in the Harlem Renaissance, including Alain Locke, Miguel Covarrubias, and Hall Johnson. Hurston's letters to both "Godmother" (as Mrs. Mason wanted her protégés to call her) and Hughes reveal how dearly both Hughes and Hurston paid for Mrs. Mason's largesse. Hughes later broke with her completely, but Hurston did not. Mrs. Mason was a rigid taskmaster who insisted on wielding unnerving control over every detail of Hurston's life, setting rigid accounting standards, and retaining power over her fieldwork. But in the end, she must be credited for recognizing Hurston's genius and sustaining her fieldwork.[27]

Hurston's perseverance in the field paid off. Although crushed by early disappointments, she plowed deeper into the fabric of Southern society as she learned to move among the people in railroad, lumber, and turpentine camps, places untouched by the larger flow of civilization. She learned to talk and dress like those among whom she collected, and to accustom herself to dangerous situations, jealous women, and barroom fights. "Primitive minds are given to sunshine and quick to anger," Hurston wrote. "Some little word, look or gesture can move them either to love or to stick a knife between your ribs. You have to sense the delicate balance and maintain it."[28] Her genius is based on her sense of this "delicate balance." She drove alone through the backwoods, packing a pistol but relying mainly on her sharp eye and quick wit.

Hurston's Barnard education and ability to find a patron were the hinges upon which her career turned, but it was her perseverance, her fortitude during trying times, that ultimately assured her success. The onset of the Great Depression heightened Hurston's struggle. It gripped the nation from the fall of 1929, when the stock market crashed, until World War II began and full employment returned. Even Godmother had felt the pinch by 1932, when the Depression bottomed out, and her financial assistance abruptly ended. As Hurston wrote in *Dust Tracks*, "The depression did away with money for research."[29]

By this time, the breadwinner in one out of every four families was out of work. State and local relief efforts crumbled under the overwhelming burden of trying to keep upward of twelve million people fed, clothed, and housed. It was at this desperate national juncture that Franklin Delano Roosevelt, the relatively unknown governor of New York, won the Presidential election of 1932, promising a defeated nation "a new deal for the American people." Change was in the wind as the federal government began taking control of relief.

More determined than ever and fearing she would never get her collection of African American folklore published, Hurston returned to Florida, subsisted on fifty cents a week for groceries lent to her by a cousin, and continued revising the collection. Publication of "The Gilded Six Bits" in *Story* magazine led to a query from publisher J. B. Lippincott: did she have a novel? She replied that she did, and began writing *Jonah's Gourd Vine*. The book's publication in 1934 led to acceptance of her folklore collection as *Mules and Men* (1935). Although her books sold (*Jonah's Gourd Vine* even became an alternate selection for the Book-of-the-Month Club), Hurston never earned enough in royalties to sustain herself financially. She continually had to seek out alternate sources of funding to keeping her writing career afloat. For a black woman in Jim Crow America, this was a difficult feat indeed.[30]

During these years, Hurston struggled constantly to make ends meet and persevered against incredible odds to establish herself as a professional writer. The ripples of her pioneering spirit would reverberate through the generation of black women writers who followed her. Margaret Walker in a 1986 interview paid Hurston the deepest compliment by noting her singular influence on her own life. "It was unheard of for a young black girl to aspire to be a writer. Only one person had even tried, and that was of course a woman from Florida, Zora Neale Hurston."[31]

II

Hurston searched continually for alternative sources of funding to keep her writing career afloat. In 1934, she worked briefly at Bethune Cookman College in Daytona Beach as a drama instructor. In early 1935, she returned to Columbia to earn her doctorate, funded by a Rosenwald Scholarship.[32] But she was bored by her Ph.D. studies, and she abandoned the attempt. Finding herself without sustenance, she frantically sought any employment she could find. Fortunately the federal government had stepped into the relief business and the New Deal of Franklin Roosevelt had launched a number of relief experiments, among them the Works Progress Administration, later named the Work Projects Administration (WPA). The WPA sponsored projects for writers, musicians, theater personnel, and artists, and black professionals like Hurston, virtually without prospects in the private sector, were able to find work in these projects—the Federal Art Project, the Federal Music Project, the Federal Theater Project, and the Federal Writers' Project.[33]

In October 1935, Hurston joined the newly organized Harlem Unit of the Federal Theater Project, where she shared company with some of the greatest names in the business, including Orson Welles, whose legendary performance of *VooDoo MacBeth* made theatrical history, and John Houseman, who codirected the unit. She did not record her feelings about the experience, but she left six months later when she received the first of two successive Guggenheim grants.

The grant funded deeper study of hoodoo, begun as early as 1927 in her fieldwork throughout the South. She intensified that inquiry in New Orleans in 1928, which she framed as an article, "Hoodoo in America," and published in *Mules and Men.*[34] But Hurston wanted to get to the root of the rituals. Jamaica and Haiti offered rich and abundant material. She remained in the Caribbean for the rest of 1936 and part of 1937 doing field work. Her persistence in the field despite warnings ended in a violent illness. (She later wrote, "For a whole day and a night, I'd thought I'd never make it.)" Terrified, she cut short her collecting and returned to New York in mid-1937.

By 1938, Hurston was living in Florida on the remainder of the second Guggenheim grant. In March she completed the manuscript that would be published that fall as *Tell My Horse.* With her book months away from publication and grant funding exhausted, she found herself in the same bleak financial position that she had experienced three years earlier while in New York, awaiting the publication of *Mules and Men.* As she had in 1935, Hurston turned to the only opportunity available for black professionals, New Deal relief. In the spring of 1938, the WPA projects were still going strong, despite mounting criticism from conservatives in Congress.[35]

Strong political pressure on the part of black leaders resulted in the hiring of black writers like Hurston. A number of aspiring writers, including Richard Wright and Ralph Ellison, got their starts on the Federal Writers' Project. In the South, Florida, Louisiana, and Virginia had instituted black writers' units—"Negro Units," as they were known colloquially. These Southern states were the only ones to sustain enough black employment to produce state African American histories. Only one was published—*The Negro in Virginia* (1940), which received laudatory reviews.[36]

There is some evidence that the Florida FWP had contacted Hurston while she was finishing the manuscript for *Tell My Horse* and asked her to be a consultant for *The Florida Negro*. She is said to have declined, citing "a heavy work schedule."[37] But months later her need for funding was acute. There remains no correspondence describing her hiring. But field representative Darel McConkey, working temporarily in the Florida state office as a troubleshooter, reported to national director Henry Alsberg that "machinery had been put in operation to add Zora Neale Hurston to the project on a security wage basis." McConkey cited her impressive credentials, her two Guggenheim Fellowships, "three or four books," and "great interest in all the project was doing."[38]

Hurston impressed her project supervisors with her "enthusiasm" and "interest," but joining a Southern writers' unit was personally challenging. It meant that despite being the toast of New York literary circles, receiving prestigious grants, and garnering solid, laudatory reviews of her books, she could not support herself. The humiliation of "going on the WPA" for middle-class persons like Hurston cannot be overemphasized. Hurston's situation was compounded by the fact that despite being the most published writer on the Florida FWP, she was forced to accept a relief rather than a supervisory position. Professional writers of Hurston's caliber were rare and ordinarily found editorial, supervisory positions at twice the relief salary of $67.50 a month that she was offered. Since most FWP personnel, especially in the South, were not professional writers, editors with writing skills and background were sought to do the actual writing that the individual project units required. Early in the program, Henry Alsberg had foreseen that "one person of writing and editorial ability will be worth fifty people without writing experience." During the early planning stages of the program, FWP administrators had built in a small nonrelief editorial quota with job security and higher wages to attract of persons with literary skills who could edit fieldworkers' copy. Unlike the Federal Art, Music, and Theater Projects, which mandated trained professionals in their respective fields, the FWP became a catchall for just about anyone who could literally write with pen and paper.[39] Architects, businessmen, pharmacists, journalists, teachers, and other white-collar workers who were unsuited to employment on the regular works programs were often assigned to the WPA's literary and research division, the FWP.

Had Hurston been given an editorial position, she would not have had to go through the lengthy and humiliating process of being "certified." Hurston had to prove her indigence by being investigated by a certification worker who visited her home and asked a number of questions about her finances. She had to swear under oath that she did not own property or have a job or draw any other means of support. Only after passing the standard "means test" could Hurston, like any other person applying for work relief, become eligible and have her name placed on a roster of "certified persons." It was from this list that the names of persons eligible for work on the Florida Federal Writers' Project were drawn.[40]

Hurston's hiring in a relief rather than an editorial-supervisory capacity was a clear-cut case of racial discrimination, and it produced repercussions. In June 1938, shortly after being hired, Hurston attended the National Folklore Festival in Washington, D.C., with a group of singers from Florida's Rollins College. While in the nation's capital, she visited FWP headquarters, where she met national director Henry Alsberg for the first time. Their conversation must have been animated by common literary and theatrical interests. He, too, held a degree from Columbia University and had been involved in New York's theatrical scene. There is little doubt that Alsberg was deeply impressed by Hurston's intelligence, wit, and charm and especially by her literary background and publishing record. After meeting Hurston, Alsberg immediately recognized in her a ready-made editor who could assist the floundering Florida staff with their stalled guidebook and African American history.[41] Florida had proved a recent thorn in the director's side. So great was the state's administrative tangle, and so lacking its editorial support, that he was forced to send Reed Harris, the FWP's assistant director, to Florida to reorganize the state office, which desperately needed persons with Hurston's background and literary skills.[42]

After meeting Hurston, Alsberg quickly wrote Florida director Carita Doggett Corse and suggested that Hurston be put in charge of editing *The Florida Negro*.[43] He proposed that in order to compensate her for this additional responsibility, her salary be raised to $150.[44] Alsberg's liberal recommendation that Hurston be made an editor sent shock waves through Florida's WPA organization, which controlled the state FWP's employment and finances. In the Southern scheme of things, blacks were not given supervisory positions, even if they were more capable or better suited. Placing an African American over whites would have violated the unwritten code of the Jim Crow South and rankled whites on the WPA and its arts projects.[45]

Florida's WPA supervisors did not follow Alsberg's recommendation. Rather than confront him directly, however, Corse sidestepped the issue and suggested that Hurston be given an additional $75 in travel allowance.[46] This would bring her salary to $142.50, close to the $150 that Alsberg had recommended. Since the highest-paid state editor earned only $160, Hurston was being paid well. But Alsberg's suggestion that she be made an editor was ignored entirely. Hurston's unfortunate experience in Florida, typical of what a black writer could expect in just about any Southern state, provides a clear example of how race and politics undermined the best interests of the Federal Writers' Project. Her ambivalent feelings about joining the FWP were magnified by the blatant racism that she had to navigate in order to collect her relief salary.[47]

Even though the Florida FWP officials denied Hurston a formal editorial position, in correspondence they often referred to her as their "Negro Editor." She herself used the title while querying several publishing houses during the spring of 1939, as she tried to get the state's African American history manuscript published.[48] But these references were little more than window dressing. True editors received nonrelief status, a higher pay scale, and job security. Hurston did not.

Understanding the Southern scheme of things, Hurston dared not protest this racial slight. She needed her relief position. Even regular WPA jobs were highly coveted political plums, and whites' demand for them far exceeded availability. Furthermore, being a field writer made it possible for her to live and work out of her own home in Eatonville, a privilege extended to only a handful of writers nationwide. For Hurston this was a far greater prize than editorial status. It enabled her to come and go as she pleased, do her own writing, and merely check in with director Corse in the state office periodically. Had Hurston been made an editor, she would have had to live and work in Jacksonville. The task of turning fieldworkers' amateur copy into publishable works would have bored her. It is not likely that Hurston would have lasted long at such a mundane, bureaucratic task.

Being left alone in Eatonville fit Hurston's artistic personality, as did her cordial, almost familial relations with her boss, Carita Doggett Corse. In Corse, the most unusual of personalities, Hurston found the ideal supervisor. She was a Southerner by birth, steeped in the region's white paternalistic outlook. But Carita Corse ventured out of her protective environment more than most Southern women would have dared. She led an active life for a wife and mother. She was a teacher, a published historian on Florida subjects, and a promoter of Florida tourism.[49] This combination of credentials made her the leading candidate for Florida's FWP directorship. She not only was recommended by literary people, but had strong political endorsement as well. Those political and social contacts proved helpful in enlisting sponsors and consultants for the project.[50]

Although Corse and Hurston came from such different backgrounds, the two women had much in common. Both had been educated in Northern colleges, had earned degrees from Columbia, and had written books about Florida; each was interested in the other's work. Hurston admired Corse's knowledge of early Florida history, while Hurston's folkloric background fascinated Corse.[51]

Hurston carefully courted Corse, treating her much as she had other powerful white women who could help her. Knowing of the project's intense interest in black studies, Hurston asked Corse to attend a "sanctified church" service. (In earlier years she had extended the same gesture to Fannie Hurst and Mrs. Mason.) Corse recalled the occasion twenty-five years later in an interview:

She [Zora] asked me one time if I would like to go visit a store front church in Jacksonville. Of course, my editors and I were delighted. So about nine o'clock one night we went down on the corner of Broad and Forsyth, further out Forsyth Street than we were accustomed to going at night as it was sort of a Negro section. And there one of the abandoned stores had been occupied as a church by the neighboring Negro congregation. We arrived about ten o'clock, and the preacher wasn't preaching very earnestly and loudly at the time, but after we took our seats, Zora whispered to me, "I'm gonna get 'em on their feet." She rose and began clapping her hands and saying in a rhythmic tone, "Yeah, Lord . . . Yes . . . Yes . . . Yes," until the rest of the congregation began to imitate her, and finally they were in such ecstasies from the hypnotic rhythm that they began to roll on the floor. I got very uneasy at this uncontrolled activity and whispered to Zora that I would like to leave. So we slipped out a side door, and took our car from the alley and departed. But it made a deep impression on me. . . .[52]

Their mutual interests and writing backgrounds helped form a solid bond between the two women. It cannot in any way be interpreted as a real friendship, for their societal roles prevented equality and neither woman was willing to cross the invisible line that separated blacks and whites. Instead, Hurston played the self-proclaimed role of "pet darkey," a guise similar to the one that she acted out with Charlotte Mason and Fannie Hurst. Today the idea seems shameful, but at the time it was a clever stratagem that Hurston used to forge a special connection with Florida's FWP director and win favors not extended to others. The curious dynamics of this relationship are spelled out in "The 'Pet' Negro System," an article Hurston wrote a few years after leaving the FWP. In it she asserted that the "South has no interest and pretends none in the mass of Negroes but is very much concerned about the individual." She pointed out that in the South, whites singled out favorite blacks, "pet negroes" as she referred to them, "for special attention and privilege." She noted, "In the unwritten Book of Dixie . . . every white man shall be allowed to pet himself a Negro. Yea, he shall take a black man unto himself to pet and to cherish, and this same Negro shall be perfect in his sight." This special attachment defied race, trouble, or strife: "Nor shall hatred among the races of man, nor conditions of strife in the walled cites, cause his pride and pleasure in his own Negro to wane."[53]

Hurston referred to herself as a "pet darkey" in a letter she wrote to Corse in December 1938, shortly after her return from a book fair in Boston and a short stopover in New York promoting the newly published *Tell My Horse:*

It would have been lovely if you had been in Boston with me. Everything was so restrained and polished that you would have been right in your element. Somehow they [the town] showed great enthusiasm for me. . . . You might have been a little proud of your pet darkey. Yes, I know that I belong to you . . . and that Sterling Brown belongs to Alsberg. You should see the little finagling he [Alsberg] does to give Sterling the edge over me. BUT he cannot make him no new head with inside trimmings and that's where he falls down. You ought to see Sterling exhibiting his jealousy as I top him time after time.[54]

By drawing attention to her warm reception in Boston and her alleged besting of national "Negro affairs editor" Sterling Brown, Hurston was building herself up in her boss's estimation. She was appealing to Corse's sensibilities, for she knew that her boss resented Brown's constant criticism of the state's insufficient coverage of African American life and the glaring errors and offensive racial comments in state copy. While Hurston's intention may have been to use "pet darkey" ironically in her letter, the irony cannot hide the element of truth in her relationship with Corse.

Corse in turn played the role of patron. Shortly after Hurston joined the project, Corse wrote Washington to obtain a recording machine for her.[55] No doubt Hurston had discussed with Corse the tremendous difference that a recorder could make in collecting folklore and mentioned a Library of Congress trip she had made three years earlier with Alan Lomax and Elizabeth Barnacle, when they had used one. Corse's requisition underscores her unusual willingness to petition the national office in Hurston's behalf and support her work.

Corse extended special privileges to Hurston in other ways. Shortly after Hurston joined the FWP, Corse invited her to visit FWP headquarters in downtown Jacksonville, an unusually liberal gesture for the times. In keeping with the strict Jim Crow code of the South, black FWP workers kept to their own office across town in the black section of the city. Black and white project workers seldom mixed. Stetson Kennedy, who worked off and on in the state office, recalled that normally the only black person ever seen at the downtown office was the runner sent over every two weeks to pick up the black writers' paychecks.

Hurston's visit to state headquarters caused a stir, one that Kennedy well remembered. He recalled Corse "calling us into her office, closing the door, and telling us that Zora was on board and would soon be paying us a visit." Corse explained to the state staff that "Hurston had been feted by New York's literary society, and had put on certain 'airs,' including the smoking of cigarettes in front of white people, and that we would all have to 'make allowances' for her. . . ." So, Kennedy added, "Zora came, and Zora smoked, and we made allowances."[56] Even more unusual was Corse's invitation to Hurston to visit her home to meet her husband, Herbert Corse, and their four children.[57]

Corse let Hurston stay in the field, requiring her presence or services only sporadically. Most FWP fieldworkers had to report daily to a nearby field office and fill out time sheets. Hurston's only requirement (one she often failed to fulfill) was to mail in her weekly assignments of 1,500 words, a task that she could complete in a day or less, leaving her the rest of the week to do her own writing. Knowing the high-quality copy she would eventually receive, Corse made allowances for Hurston's artistic personality, condoning her erratic work habits, her periodic writing lapses, her all too frequent disappearances, and her unmet deadlines. As Corse explained in a 1976 interview, "She [Hurston] would go off and you wouldn't know where she was and she was supposed to be working by the week."[58] After these lapses, Hurston would suddenly appear at state headquarters or else frame a heartfelt letter offering her apologies and a host of excuses. One of these letters survives, showing the way in which Hurston finagled her way back into her boss's good graces:

I am sitting down this time to write you a much-felt letter, Boss. I am risking it because you are an author yourself and I feel that you can understand my form of insanity perhaps. Dr., every now and then I get a sort of phobia for paper and all its works. I cannot bring myself to touch it. I cannot write, read or do anything at all for a period. . . . I have just been through one of those periods that lasted about nine days. It is stronger than I am boss. But when I do come out of it, I am as if I had just been born again.[59]

The privilege of working out of her home in Eatonville without visible ties to the WPA enabled Hurston to ask the true nature of her employment and keep up appearances. Years later when asked about her aunt's relief position on the FWP, Winifred Hurston knew nothing, even though she had lived with her aunt at the time. Hurston's Maitland post office address might have been part of the guise as well.[60]

Hurston's relief check was generous enough that she could help support Wilhelmina and Winifred Hurston, her now deceased brother Bob's daughters. Sometime after September 1937, Hurston invited Wilhelmina, Robert's eldest daughter and a young woman of twenty just starting out on her own, to come and live with her in Eatonville. Hurston was especially close to Wilhelmina, whom she had cared for as a child. Winifred was also very close to her aunt. Hurston had visited Memphis frequently when both of them were growing up.

Nothing in Winifred's growing-up years equaled the excitement when Aunt Zora came to town. Winifred recalled that the family never knew when Zora might suddenly appear. "She would just leave and you couldn't hear from her for a long time, and then the next thing you knew she might pop up to visit for a few days," Winifred asserted. When she arrived, word quickly spread through the Scott Street neighborhood: "Doc's sister's here! Doc's sister's here!" The neighbors would gather to listen to her and admire her clothes. She was invited to speak at church, an opportunity extended only to important individuals. Hurston's silk pajama outfits made an indelible impression on the little girls in the neighborhood, who tried to imitate her by wearing their sleeping pajamas to the corner store. They were chagrined when the store owner asked, "Did you just get out of the bed? You can't do just like Zora!" Hurston's presence kept the school bullies at bay when her nieces and nephews, capitalizing on the well-known fact that Zora carried a pearl-handled revolver, announced on the school grounds, "Don't bother us anymore. Our aunt is up here with a pistol." The ploy worked and the Hurston children enjoyed a reprieve. "But after Zora left," Mrs. Clark added, "they tore us up!"[61]

Wilhelmina loved Eatonville and wrote her sister Winifred back in Memphis about the good times that she was having. And indeed she was. While there, Wilhelmina met John Hamilton, known by the nickname "Seaboard," who was reputed to be the fastest orange picker in Orange County. Seaboard became a frequent visitor, and in August 1938 he married Wilhelmina.[62]

Once Wilhelmina married, Hurston extended a similar invitation to Winifred, who had just graduated from high school in Memphis and was working in her Uncle Ben's pharmacy. Winifred jumped at the opportunity to follow in her sister's footsteps.[63]

While working on the FWP, Hurston lived on the edge of Eatonville at the crossroads known as Tuxedo Junction, a name which recalls a popular jukebox tune of the times and reflects the earlier use of Hurston's dwelling as a nightclub. Hurston had chosen the location because it offered solitude as well as beauty and inspiration. The house, which had once been a barn, stood on the bank of one of the many lakes in the area, amid a magnificent setting of massive oaks dripping with Spanish moss. The pristine beauty of the place so struck federal writer Paul Diggs, who visited Hurston there, that he judged it "an ideal setting for a country lodge."[64]

It was here in this location in central Florida, a place to which she was compulsively drawn, that Hurston found the inspiration and peace she needed to write her fifth novel, *Moses: Man of the Mountain*, as well as to turn out her Federal Writers' Project assignments. Winifred recalled her aunt's habits while writing and offered a rare glimpse of Hurston at work. She noted that while working on a manuscript, Hurston stayed relatively close to home. "Most of the time she was there at night," Winifred remembered. "Sometimes she would go out. Mostly she'd stay around the house. When she did go out, she'd go to Winter Park . . . to Rollins College . . . or she played croquet with a white woman in Maitland." She often moved her typewriter, a card table, and a chair outdoors and wrote under the trees, dressed in coveralls. She stayed there all day, talked to no one, and everyone knew to leave her alone." Winifred noted that writing days like these were interspersed with research and reading.

Hurston created a comfortable, homelike setting for herself and her nieces. She cooked for them every night, serving meals so delicious that Winifred readily recalled her aunt's culinary skills decades later. The girls were enthralled by their aunt's impetuous nature and unpredictable behavior, which contrasted sharply with their strict Memphis upbringing. Winifred vividly recalls one episode. One day, her aunt approached her with the simple question "Do you want to go and see your Uncle John?" Winifred voiced her approval of the idea, thinking they would plan the trip to Jacksonville and leave in a few days. But to Winifred's amazement, Zora said, "Get ready, let's go." With that the pair made a whirlwind trip, staying but a few hours and returning the same day. Much to her niece's chagrin, Hurston wore her coveralls on the trip.

Treating her nieces like trusted daughters, Hurston left them in charge of the house and lent them her car when she had to go out of town. Evidently she preferred to take the bus when she made her frequent trips to FWP headquarters in Jacksonville. At these times she would announce to Winifred, "I've got to go to New York for a few days." Winifred would drive her aunt to the local bus station, drop her off, and keep her aunt's car until she returned. "I know I kept her car a lot in those days," Winifred recalled.[65]

These trips to "New York" were doubtless a ruse to conceal Hurston's FWP employment. In the 1930s, New York was a two-day bus ride. More than likely Hurston was traveling on FWP assignments around the state or to Jacksonville to check in with Carita Corse at FWP headquarters.

III

Hurston brought to the Federal Writers' Project the mature talent of a seasoned writer and folklorist. By the late 1930s, she had come very far from her early field days when as a naive student she cried before Franz Boas, fearing her awesome mentor was displeased with her field efforts.[66] *Mules and Men* had established her reputation as a folklorist.[67] Her collecting in 1936 and 1937 in Jamaica and Haiti for the book that would become *Tell My Horse* (1938) deepened her ability as a field collector and knowledge as an anthropologist. It was on this trip that Hurston stumbled on the secret of the zombies, a pioneering discovery for which she was given little credit and which paved the way years later for Harvard ethnologist Wade Davis to identify the secret substance used by natives to simulate death.[68]

Hurston's formidable talents would now be applied to the FWP's folklore program. Hurston's enrollment on the Florida FWP coincided judiciously with the hiring of Benjamin A. Botkin as the FWP's first full-time folklore director. In Botkin, Hurston would find a like-minded colleague who deeply respected her fieldwork and used her talents to both redirect and enlarge the FWP program.

More than anyone else, Botkin shaped the positive direction that the FWP folklore program would take. He had the impressive academic and publishing credentials that the FWP desperately needed to win the support of academic sponsors like the American Folklore Society. His undergraduate degree was from Harvard. He had done graduate work at Columbia University and earned a Ph.D. in English from the University of Nebraska. While still an undergraduate at Harvard, Botkin developed his lifelong fascination with folklore, an interest he greatly expanded while serving as an English instructor at the University of Oklahoma. By the early 1930s he had edited several volumes as *Folk-Say: A Regional Miscellany*. This publication defined his interest in "living lore," present and dynamic folk life, and "folk-say," what people have to say about themselves. When offered a chance to expand his horizons and direct an effort to produce national publications, Botkin jumped at the opportunity. He joined the FWP in May 1938, believing that he was participating in "the greatest educational as well as social experiment of our time." In the FWP he saw an even greater chance "to give back to the people what we have taken from them and what rightfully belongs to them."[69]

Upon taking the helm of the FWP folklore program, Botkin expanded collection efforts and plans for publications. Whereas early efforts concentrated on more traditional folklore, Botkin encouraged the collection of contemporary and urban lore in order to broaden understanding of America's cultural fabric. He believed folklore could help Americans achieve a deeper understanding of the nation's multicultural context. He stressed the living relationship between folklore and the cultural context, "relating the foreground of lore to its background in life." To Botkin, folklore was ever changing, ever growing, and ever emerging. Many of these ideas are framed in the nineteen-page *Manual for Folklore Studies* that he compiled shortly after he joined the project.[70] With Botkin guiding national folkloric efforts, Hurston's field efforts were heightened. And those efforts would first be directed toward adding imaginative and colorful African American lore to Florida's automotive guidebook.[71]

Hurston joined the Florida FWP just as the final rewrite of the state's guidebook was taking place and the need for experienced writers was especially acute. In Florida, most delays had been caused by lack of good writers. It had taken state editors two years to get the guidebook's first two sections, "Essays" and "Cities," complete. And now national FWP editors had returned the Florida tour section, "The Florida Loop," to state editors, judging most of them "dull and lifeless" and ordering that they be rewritten. Greater insight and imagination as well as more incisive description of Florida's background and history were needed. Few Florida FWP workers had proved adept at the task. The national FWP wanted material that would provide a "fresh firsthand viewpoint" of not only the highway vistas one would expect along the routes, but of regional variations, local history, and lore.[72] Just before Hurston was enrolled on the Florida FWP, the national office had sent national field representative Darel McConkey to Florida to help the state staff organize their tour section. Although McConkey's field reports back to Washington are filled with insightful analysis, the real problem was the lack of good field writers. It was at this point of greatest need that Zora Neale Hurston appeared. Not only was Hurston a proven writer, but McConkey expected her to "add valuable new Florida folklore to the guide."[73]

Hurston went to work immediately writing folklore for the tours section of the Florida guidebook. Guide instructions cautioned field writers "to survey their districts with 'fresh eyes' and recognize the lore and customs known to them all of their lives." For the purposes of the guides, the FWP wanted folk customs that could be tied to "one place, one section, or one object."[74] Following these instructions, Hurston crafted her African American lore to fit guidebook specifications. Judging from the time frame and the copy she submitted, it is almost certain that she did not go out into the field to do any new collecting, but dipped into her files and drew material from her concentrated collecting expeditions throughout the South during the 1927–31 period. Her folklore vignettes targeted Florida topics such as the all-night roar of alligators and how the land turtle got its name. Some of this material derived from her childhood; some, whether peculiar to Florida or from elsewhere in the South, she had discovered in her earlier collecting. Several of her stories resemble those found in *Mules and Men.* Others were entirely new.

Placing Hurston's folkloric tales in the tour's geographical context sharpened their meaning while at the same time heightening their interest. The group of stories lumped together as "Negro Mythical Places," representing for the most part new and vibrant folklore, illustrates this point well. Credited to the state's turpentiners, the stories were situated in the guidebook's automotive tour through northern Florida, where thousands of black turpentiners lived and worked. As some of the South's most deprived laborers, these men could only dream of places like "Diddy-Wah-Diddy," a magical destination where neither man nor beast had to worry about work or food. Both were magically supplied. They often laughed and dreamed of far-off "Heaven," pinning human qualities on its celestial inhabitants. Here would-be angels were sent back down to earth because they displayed human qualities. Similarly, "West Hell" and "Beluthahatchee" described mythical retreats where the inhabitants acted out human foibles. One can easily discern how the telling of these stories of devilment and delight lifted heavy hearts. Hurston's folktales not only demonstrated local lore, but aptly illustrated the creativity and versatility of "the Negro farthest down."[75]

Hurston more than likely knew that the tales' deeper meanings would escape the guide's white readership. But she sensed the opportunity of getting into the FWP guidebook the African American point of view. Therefore the tales she selected for the Florida guidebook bear special emphasis. They were two-edged swords. On the surface level, the reader is presented with lively stories that conjure vivid images of heaven, hell, magical food, and singing streets. Yet on a deeper level, the tales reveal encoded messages speaking of resistance. Some address the wisdom and wit of the group pointed at the devil/white man. Others voiced thoughts on coping with the color line. Still others admonished blacks to follow directions, for it was a white man's world. In short, the tales' encoded messages show Hurston was signifying, "resisting whites' intrusions into black affairs."[76] She purposely chose powerful characters like "Big John de Conquer," who she knew were culture heroes that downtrodden blacks had used for years to symbolize their triumph over poverty, want, deprivation, and the full effects of a racist society. She likewise chose others who urged patience and forgiveness, exemplified humor, or spoke of a better world. Thus Hurston's folkloric characters mirror the varied realities of African American lives.

Hurston added town histories to the Florida tours, as well. These were thumbnail sketches of places along the tour route that were meant to encapsulate, in a paragraph or two, the life spirit of the towns that the tourist/travelers passed. Most town histories were compiled in the state office from fieldworkers' notes. Few ended up intact as did Hurston's, easily recognized, without extensive editing. Hurston's town histories enabled her to put forth the African American point of view. Her first, "Eatonville as You Look at It," voiced residents' feelings about the significance of their town: the landmarks and edifices, churches, stories, and drinking places that gave it communal life. Her write-ups of the Ocoee incident and the once vibrant all-black township of Goldsborough showed those residents' feelings about ugly racial incidents. Also found in the Florida state guide under the town history of Pahokee was a fully credited excerpt from *Their Eyes Were Watching God.*

Hurston completed her guidebook writing by the end of the summer, for the final manuscript had been forwarded to the Washington office that fall. Typically one or two members of the state staff assisted national editors in their preparation of the book for publication. Two state editors, Max Hunter and Rolland Phillips, traveled to Washington to do the final edit of the book. Interestingly enough, Zora Neale Hurston was sent as well. The state office had not sent her. Washington had requested her, proving that the more liberal national office supported broader inclusion of the multicultural point of view expressed in Hurston's folklore studies and town histories.

Once the editing of the state's guidebook was complete, the Florida FWP turned its attention toward a host of auxiliary publications. Foremost among them was Florida's African American publication, a project that would consume the greater part of Hurston's writing for the Florida FWP.

IV

Like most other New Deal programs, interest in black culture grew out of political considerations. By 1935, Franklin Roosevelt had taken to heart the fact that the black vote could swing the election in seventeen important northern cities. From this point forward, and with the decided leadership of first lady Eleanor Roosevelt, New Deal programs began exploring ways of increasing employment possibilities for blacks. Black advisers were added to federal agencies. These men in turn created their own informal study/pressure group that came to be known as the "Black Cabinet." Headed by Florida's own Mary McLeod Bethune, they focused on ways of increasing black employment in New Deal programs.[77]

Racial inequities in the states, steady pressure on the part of black leaders, and the growing realization of the power of the black vote worked together to forge more liberal hiring of African Americans. By 1935, with his reelection campaign looming, FDR took notice, and New Deal programs, especially the WPA, began hiring blacks in increasing numbers. The WPA's inclusion of blacks led eventually to the hiring of black professionals on its arts projects. In the Federal Writers' Project, national director Henry Alsberg, who was by all counts an open and caring liberal, began exploring ways of increasing black employment and the broadcasting the African American point of view.[78]

At the urging of prominent black leaders, Sterling Brown, a thirty-five-year-old Howard University English professor and poet with a deep grounding in African American literature, agreed to serve as the

Federal Writers' Project's part-time Negro affairs editor. In this national advisory capacity, he was to oversee and ensure adequate coverage of African American history in the guides. However, knowing from the start that in the South, state directors would be reluctant to cover African American history and life adequately, he planned an ambitious national study, "The Portrait of the Negro as an American," to chronicle black history as a part of the larger American experience.[79]

While the national office deliberated ways of increasing coverage of African American life in the guides, financial resources were being sought to increase black employment in a number of Southern states. Whites simply refused to work in the company of blacks. As a result, the New Deal appropriated the funds to set up separate "Negro Units" in several states. In January 1936, Louisiana's employment quota was increased so that fifteen black writers could be hired. In Florida in March 1936, ten black writers were employed.[80] These included Martin Richardson, J. M. Johnson, Alfred Farrell, Winston Rice, Rebecca Baker, Viola Muse, Rachel Austin, Pearl Randolph, and Grace Thompson, who began researching the state's African American roots. Although the unit was based in Jacksonville, Florida's black writers ranged all over the state. Viola Muse covered the Tampa area, and Rebecca Baker canvassed Daytona. Paul Diggs, who joined in 1938, would center his research in central and southwestern Florida.[81]

In Florida, the black writers fanned out across the state. Martin Richardson paid a visit to Pensacola, interviewing local residents, pastors of black churches, and former slaves. J. M. Johnson did the same in Jacksonville and St. Augustine. Alfred Farrell covered the Tallahassee area, and others combed Jacksonville, Tampa, and Daytona Beach. These black writers appeared with pen and paper in conjure shops to list herbs and cures. They eavesdropped in barbershops to record local gossip. They visited shops to learn more about the gambling game bolita. They attended funerals and documented local burial practices. They attended services in storefront churches—"sanctified churches"—and wrote about them. They talked with everyone—dock workers, funeral attendants, barbers, black leaders, and outstanding personalities. They found ex-slaves who were willing to tell tales of their bondage.[82] Nothing of interest was overlooked.

By 1937, the writers had amassed enough research to begin writing the African American history of Florida. Of the ten black writers hired, only Martin Richardson was allowed to write any of the proposed chapters. Richardson completed "Slave Days in Florida," the introductory chapter, which drew heavily on the ex-slaves' interviews. The remainder of the loosely compiled 167-page manuscript consisted of a hundred pages of rough, unedited field copy detailing the African American histories of Florida's major cities and including ethnic studies of Pensacola, Jacksonville, and St. Augustine.[83]

This was the status of Florida's African American history project when Zora Neale Hurston came on board in April 1938. Although the writers' research was indeed impressive, a person with a strong literary background was needed to fashion their raw field copy into a publishable work. The national office wanted Zora Neale Hurston to do just this. Florida's FWP director, however, had other designs.

There is no way of knowing whether Hurston's arrival had any influence on the move to extend the book, but during the summer of 1938, the outline for the "Negro Book" was enlarged and new chapters on folklore, music, art, and literature were added. Hurston was put in charge of writing these new chapters as well as additions to the chapters on religion and amusements.

All indications are that Hurston began her writing assignments for the book with the folklore and music essay. In sharp contrast to her writing for the state guidebook, Hurston was left largely to her own devices. Without the strict confines of guidebook writing, she could draw more subjectively on her background as an anthropologist and folklorist and her creativity as a writer. She produced a masterful essay centered on the theme of primitive man's need to create folklore to explain the world around him. The essay discusses folklore's development, the various forms it takes in song and prose, and its significance to the culture and includes copious examples. In final form, "Go Gator and Muddy the Water" is a veritable treasury of African American folklore.

Hurston was also asked to contribute a chapter detailing Florida blacks' contributions to the arts. This simple assignment—one which Hurston was readily equipped to do, for she knew most of Florida's black writers, artists, and musicians personally—drew from her a startling piece. Instead of tracing the artistic and literary contributions of Florida blacks, Hurston launched into a heated charge that blacks' progress in the arts had been held back. In this essay, titled "Art and Such," she wrote just what she wanted, infusing her own opinion, something FWP writers were cautioned never to do. Although it ill served the FWP's purposes, the essay is a fascinating discussion of how, in Hurston's opinion, race politics retarded black literature and the arts.

Why had Hurston turned from a simple summary of black Floridians' contributions to the arts in favor of an extended discussion of how African Americans' creativity had been thwarted? The time of the essay's writing and its literary argument provide clues that deeper motives were operative. "Art and Such" is Hurston's stout defense of her own literary point of view, which by the late 1930s was under vehement attack. Other blacks, especially writers, who did not understand her work felt that her focus on the beauty of black culture ran against the racial politics of the day.

Using the podium available, Hurston was delivering a stout counterattack against her most vehement critics. Although it is a matter of speculation, it is very possible she was directing her essay toward two of them in particular, national Negro affairs editor Sterling Brown and fellow writer and FWP colleague Richard Wright. Wright joined the FWP in Chicago in late 1935, and later transferred to the New York unit. While on the FWP, Wright won a *Story* magazine contest and instant recognition as the most promising young writer on the Federal Writers' Project. Wright was working on the novel that would be published as *Native Son* (1940) and would catapult him to fame and success as a writer.[84]

Both Wright and Sterling Brown had written scathing reviews of Hurston's novel *Their Eyes Were Watching God* (1937). Writing in *The Nation*, Brown had chided Hurston for her lack of racial focus. He questioned Hurston's characters' lack of racial bitterness and their seemingly carefree and easy manner. He believed Eatonville a poor representation of black life, pointing out its exceptional character: "Living in an all-colored town, these people escape the worst pressures of class and caste. There is little harshness; here there is enough money and work to go around."[85]

Brown's comments had to have hurt. As an author, scholar, and critic, he carried weight. Now not only was he technically her superior, but he had also found a firm place in the establishment and literary mainstream, claims that Hurston could not make for herself. In addition, Brown was now a New Deal insider. On an FWP administrative flow chart he would appear as the final editor of the Florida African American history project. Did Hurston write "Art and Such" for Sterling Brown to read? More than likely she did. However, the essay was never forwarded to Washington. Copies of it are found only in state archives. All evidence points to the fact that Brown never read the essay, nor any part of the manuscript for *The Florida Negro*, for that matter. By the time the manuscript was completed and circulated in the state office, Brown was on administrative leave.[86]

Hurston may also have written "Art and Such" to answer Richard Wright's review of *Their Eyes Were Watching God*, published in *New Masses*. Wright penned what must have been one of the most brutal reviews of any of Hurston's books. He asserted that the "sensory sweep of the novel carries no theme, no message" and accused Hurston of following the "minstrel technique that makes the 'white folks' laugh. Her characters eat and laugh and cry and work and kill; they swing like a pendulum eternally in that safe and narrow orbit in which America likes to see the Negro live: between laughter and tears."[87] In "Art and Such," Hurston counters with the argument that black writers need to go beyond the simplistic view of race put forth by race leaders, or "race champions" as she calls them, and begin to explore the beauty and integrity of black culture. Her characters speak "to the song of morning" rather than to the "sorrow and suffering of the race."

Hurston completed a number of other writing assignments for the project that were to serve as additions to existing chapters. The first of these, her essay on black folk religion, "The Sanctified Church," was to be a part of the chapter on religion. This assignment resulted in one of her most brilliant essays. The background circumstances of its writing are worthy of examination, for they underscore how the FWP inspired her writings.

When Hurston joined the FWP, she found in black writers' unit files a number of pieces on black religion. Viola Muse had written an eight-page commentary on a sanctified church in Tampa. Based largely on interviews with church members and personal observation, it documented the church's founding, growth, and religious practices.[88] Less balanced and more critical were investigations by Martin Richardson, J. M. Johnson, and Winston Rice of storefront churches in Jacksonville.[89] Their middle-class disdain for the communicants' unusual practices—the "call-and-response" shouts between preacher and congregation, the free-form dancing, the unorthodox music—and for the churches' fluctuating memberships skewed the credibility of their work.

Hurston had long been interested in these folk churches. As early as 1929, she had written of her experiences and impressions involving "some of the variations on the Protestant theme like the sanctified." She pointed out that these churches were important as an explanation of "the revolt against the sterile rituals of the Protestant churches and a reversion to paganism."[90] As an anthropologist, she understood religion, which expressed the people's most sacred values and the meaning that they gave their lives. It was in the sanctified churches that Hurston discovered what she believed to be the purest expressions of African American culture. Her continuing fascination with the subject of folk religion and the symbiotic relation of the preacher to the congregation forms a continuous theme through her writing, emerging first in *Jonah's Gourd Vine* (1934) and in "Spirituals and Neo-Spirituals" in *Negro: An Anthology* (1934).

Sparked by the FWP reports, seeking perhaps to enlarge or correct them, Hurston wrote "The Sanctified Church." It remains a seminal and deeply analytical treatise that summarizes her views on the subject. Considered in the context of the times in which it was written, "The Sanctified Church" shows that Hurston was years ahead of her time in linking African tribal practices with African American religion.

In addition to inspiring the writing of "The Sanctified Church," it is quite possible that the FWP motivated Hurston's further study of these churches. While working on the Florida FWP, Hurston was in contact with her old friend and colleague Jane Belo, organizing what would become a study of a sanctified church in Beaufort, South Carolina. After leaving the FWP, Hurston traveled there, interviewed the church membership, and recorded religious practices in detail. Her study is enshrined in a twenty-five-page study titled "Ritualistic Expression from the Lips of the Communicants of the Seventh Day Church of God." It contains interviews with eight communicants, focused on "exact descriptions of the trance," and details the splitting of "two churches complete with intrigue, love interest, etc."[91]

"The Sanctified Church" remains the most widely known of Hurston's FWP writings. First published in 1981 in the collection of her folklore work titled *The Sanctified Church*, it has deeply influenced the work of modern scholars. Eric Sundquist, citing the essay as one of Hurston's most important pieces on African American culture, mentions Hurston's early recognition of the African in communal performances, most notably the call-and-response interplay between preacher and congregation, singing, and dance.[92]

The FWP drew from Hurston pieces on other aspects of black culture that she otherwise might not have written. Hurston had long been interested in children's games and their deeper implications as a reflection of black culture. The FWP's broad folkloric interest in them— Abbot Ferris collected them in Mississippi[93] and Herbert Halpert recorded them in 1939 for the WPA's Southeast Recording Expedition— gave her ample opportunity to write more extensively about them. The result would be "New Children's Games," an insightful essay that included, as did her other FWP essays, copious examples to illustrate her points. More than likely, "New Children's Games" was intended as a part of the "Amusements" chapter of *The Florida Negro*. Hurston divides the games into three categories: those black children borrowed from whites, some they modified to their own uses, and others that she believed had been brought from Africa. She had mentioned some of these games in *Mules*, most notably the rhyming games known as "Going 'Round de Mountain," "Little Sally Walker," "Sissy in de Barn," and "Chick, Mah Chick, Mah Craney Crow." In "New Children's Games" she appraises their meaning, cites their significance to African American culture, and points out that these play tunes reflect the "serious activities" of grown-ups and mirror the major characteristic of black culture, "the will to rhythm."[94]

By late spring 1939, Hurston had finished her essays for the *The Florida Negro*.[95] At this time, she sent out query letters to several commercial publishers describing the Florida book's "unusual and colorful material" and asking if they would be interested in seeing the manuscript. At least one editor showed interest, but most publishers declined, citing tight depression budgets and shrinking book markets. The truth of the matter was that despite Hurston's glowing description of the manuscript, *The Florida Negro* was not in publishable form in 1939. Deeper research, tighter organization, and extensive editing would have made it a passable work, but in no way would the book have compared with the FWP's *The Negro in Virginia* (1940).

Although Hurston had written extensively for *The Florida Negro*, in the end none of her essays would be included in it. After she left the project in 1939, white editors in the state office continued revision of the state's African American study. Letters Hurston wrote to publishers, the book's point of view, and Stetson Kennedy's testimony indicate that Carita Corse did much of the editing herself.[96]

While Corse supervised the revision of the manuscript, Stetson Kennedy and Robert Cornwall both worked on it. It was at this juncture that Kennedy penned "No Race Champion," an essay that challenged Hurston's ideas about race expressed in "Art and Such." Hurston's ideology rankled Cornwall and Kennedy, who championed the race position of Richard Wright and others. They deleted all of Hurston's writings from the final manuscript, which was finally published in 1993 as *The Florida Negro: A Federal Writers' Project Legacy*.

V

During her last months on the Florida FWP, Hurston's role as a federal writer broadened considerably as she was taken from behind the scenes and given a larger, more public presence. The FWP needed her skills as a dramatist to publicize the FWP's activities in the state and stave off Congressional attempts to terminate the arts projects. By late 1938, the New Deal's political position had eroded considerably in Congress. To diehard conservatives, the idea of the federal government directly sponsoring the arts seemed frivolous and foolhardy, and when they could muster the political power, as they slowly began to do by 1938, they worked to terminate the arts projects entirely.

The strongest indication of the conservative backlash in Congress was the formation of the House Committee on Un-American Activities. During the summer of 1938, just about the time that Hurston was settling into her duties as a federal writer, the newly formed committee was beginning its long and varied career as Communist witch-hunter and baiter. Led by Rep. Martin Dies of Texas, an archconservative anti–New Dealer, the committee began hearings that concocted charges against the WPA arts projects. These unsubstantiated charges were aired in the media and hurt the public image of the FWP.[97]

As the sensational newspaper headlines continued, the New Dealers had no choice but to fight back. As consummate politicians, they knew that one of the most effective ways to counteract the Dies Committee's charges would be to generate grassroots support. Public approval would pressure state Congressional delegations and perhaps save the arts projects.

In Florida, the WPA's arts and education programs planned a public demonstration of their achievements.[98] With the future of the arts projects in grave danger, Corse called on Hurston to stage a demonstration of Florida folklore. Everyone loved a show, and judging from her past successes, Corse knew that Hurston could present a first-class one.[99]

The choice of the Orlando location for the production could well have been a concession to Hurston, who lived but a few miles away in Eatonville and could draw the show's dancers, singers, and musicians from her local contacts. Winifred Hurston Clark remembers a number of young people coming to Eatonville and staying in local homes, and her aunt teaching them dances. These activities had to have been the background preparations for the WPA production.[100] Although the program pamphlet speaks of "The Fire Dance" as an example of "the new national folklore studies of the Federal Writers' Project," in reality, it was a recreation of the midnight scene from Hurston's 1932 off-Broadway production, "The Great Day."[101]

Hurston staged two performances of "The Fire Dance," one in mid-January and the other in mid-February. These African tribal rites welcoming spring were the same dances which Hurston had collected in the Bahamas in the late 1920s. They originated in Africa, where they had been performed in the nude. The best description of them can be found in Hurston's 1930 article in the *Journal of American Folklore*:

There are two kinds of the dance, the jumping dance, and the ring play, which is merely a more elaborate form of the jumping dance. In either form of this dancing, the players form a ring, with the bonfire to one side. The drummer usually takes his place near the fire. The drum is held over the blaze until the skin tightens to the right tone. There is a flourish signifying that the drummer is all set. The players begin to clap with their hands. The drummer cries, "Gimbay!" (a corruption of the African word *gumbay*, a large drum) and begins the song. He does not always select the song. The players more often call out what they want played. One player is inside the ring. He or she does his preliminary flourish, which comes on the first line of the song, does his dance on the second line, and chooses his successor on the third line and takes his place in the circle. The chosen dancer takes his place and the dance goes on until the drum gets cold.[102]

For the FWP program, Hurston found slim teenagers to dance the parts. She knew that the graceful vision of the young dancers arrayed in colorful costumes moving to the rhythmic beat of the drums would entertain without shocking the white middle-class audiences. Hurston's judgment was correct. Local crowds responded enthusiastically, and she earned the effusive praise of Dr. Corse. Years later Corse remembered Hurston's cleverness in an interview: "Zora was smart enough to get young, slender fourteen-year-olds, tall and graceful, for her dances. So while they were true, the true motions of the spring rites, they were graceful and only slightly suggestive. In older people they would have been quite shocking.[103]

Knowing the agenda at hand, Hurston had modified her program to fit her audience's taste. She had succeeded admirably. But her Bahamian dances could not counter the insurmountable forces that were moving against the FWP. These larger pressures were far too powerful to have been stopped by African-derived dances performed in Florida's citrus belt.

Hurston's first field assignment took her from behind the scenes and thrust her into the state arena. Her second, as field scout and organizer for the WPA Joint Committee on Folk Art's recording expedition, would bring her national attention and put her back into the Florida folkloric field that she knew and loved so well. The Joint Committee on Folk Art, formed shortly after Ben Botkin took over as the head of the FWP's folklore program, needed Hurston's help in arranging the Florida leg of its southeast recording trip. Some time earlier, Botkin called together representatives from the WPA's Federal Writers', Music, Art, Theater, and Educational Projects to form the Joint Committee on Folk Art. As its first endeavor, the Joint Committee planned a trip through the Southeast to record the local lore that state FWP projects had discovered. Simple written transcriptions of songs and stories had proved a less than satisfactory means of preserving them. What was needed was actual recordings in the voices of informants to replicate accent, intonation, and dialect, as well as the background music. These sounds were just as important as the words.[104]

Florida promised vibrant material. John Lomax, who had preceded Botkin as national folklore director, had traveled through the state during the spring of 1937 and spent several weeks making records of folk songs. His efforts, however, had barely scratched the surface.[105] As one of the nation's most economically and ethnically diversified areas, Florida was filled with the songs and lore of all types of laborers. African American dockworkers sang as they loaded and unloaded boats along the wharfs of Jacksonville's busy harbor. Railroad hands heaved and then hammered down 700-pound steel rails to the rhythmic cries of special callers. In south Florida, Bahamian migrants who had come to cut sugarcane enriched the area with their exotic drum music, song, and dance. In Tampa and Key West, Latin cigar workers flavored the towns with their old-world customs, songs, and stories. Similarly, the Greek sponge fishermen of Tarpon Springs and Portuguese fishermen of St. Augustine left their ethnic imprint on these coastal towns.[106]

With so much material, a plan was needed to coordinate Florida recording efforts. Botkin knew Hurston could formulate one for the Joint Committee trip, of which Florida was to be the last leg. The national folklore director's request drew from Hurston a compelling seven-page narrative, "Proposed Recording Expedition into the Floridas," that presented a summation of Florida's distinct folkloric offerings.[107]

Hurston suggested unusual people for the recorders to interview, like "Pap" Drummond of Fernandina Beach, who told tales about pirates and buried treasure. She identified her own field interests in south Florida, an area that she believed contained the most ethnically diverse folkloric material in the entire South, and she invited the recorders to follow in her footsteps. Hurston's report foreshadows her own recording interests, which she would pursue less than a year later in Beaufort, South Carolina. Nowhere is Hurston's brilliance as an anthropologist clearer than in this concise analysis of "the inner melting pot of the great melting pot—America." It very easily could have stood as the folklore essay in the state guidebook, which paled in comparison with Hurston's masterful analysis and consummate literary style.

Once her report for the impending recording expedition was complete, Corse sent Hurston to Cross City to line up informants for the recordings. Here in this isolated hamlet in the northwestern part of the state, modern life had barely intruded. It was areas such as these, untouched by contemporary influences such as the phonograph and the radio, that offered the best possibilities of gathering unusual lore, customs, work songs, stories, and sayings.[108]

Although by the late 1930s the turpentine industry was beginning to play out in the state, Florida still produced up to 20 percent of the world supply. Thousands of Floridians lived and worked in the remote piney woods, without running water or any other trappings of modern life. Most of these turpentiners and their families were uneducated. They left few written accounts of their lives. Their folklore was one of the few barometers of their attitudes and feelings about themselves.

Most turpentine operators in Florida and elsewhere closed their camps to strangers. They did not want outsiders, especially government outsiders, stirring up their people. Most of them worked under the worst labor conditions in the state, including peonage. In a most unusual gesture, the Aycock and Lindsay Company, headquartered in Cross City, had agreed to open its doors to FWP researchers. Its far-flung operation, which covered fifteen camps spread across two counties and distilling plants in Cross City, employed some three hundred turpentiners and their dependents, some fifteen hundred people in all.

Aycock and Lindsay's unusual candidness can only be attributed to the company's part owner and operating manager, Catherine Lindsay. Catherine Lindsay was the widow of B. H. Lindsay, one of the company's founders. After his death, "Miss Catherine," as she was known to everyone in the area from the lowliest dipper to the town's mayor, had taken over Mr. Lindsay's interests, and she ran the company's day-to-day operations. By all accounts she was a strikingly beautiful woman who combined her wily feminine charms with her astute business sense to achieve commanding results. The turpentiners both loved and feared her. Her male partners bowed to her wishes. She ruled with an iron glove. Because she exercised life-and-death control over the camps, she had no qualms or misgivings about giving federal writers access to her workers.[109]

In addition to serving as "advanced scout" for the WPA recorders and meeting with Miss Catherine, Hurston was to coordinate the arrival of two FWP staff members, state editor William Duncan and photographer Robert Cook, who were being sent to Cross City to do a story on turpentining. Hurston, who was immediately struck with Miss Catherine, wrote the men a glowing description of her. Duncan later admitted that he fully expected a "breakdown" in Hurston's depiction of "this remarkable person" and that he and Bob Cook "were on the alert." But as the two men swiftly learned when they met her in person, Hurston had not done Miss Catherine sufficient justice. They were taken with her beauty, wit, charm, and intellect. In his Cross City report, Duncan wrote:

> She directs the entire business of the largest turpentine plant in Florida in America's last frontier, West Florida, an area largely populated by escaped felons and fugitives from justice during its early days. Even today it is untouched. . . . Miss Catherine, herself, sleeps with the certain comfort of a .38-caliber revolver in arm's reach, on her windowsill, two double-barreled shotguns in the corner of the room and a .22 automatic rifle and a 16-gauge shotgun just inside the front door. She said she had used them on occasion, too.[110]

Once she had coordinated arrangements for Duncan and Cook, Hurston was left to her own devices. The two men were off driving with

Miss Catherine, who explained turpentine operations and showed them the various camps. Hurston sensed her privilege in being allowed to roam the Aycock and Lindsay operations and gather information about one of the state's most famous and infamous trades. She recorded in her field notes that her appearance in remote Cross City touched a raw nerve in the people. "The people murmured at me with the edge of their lips," she wrote.[111] The whole experience deeply impressed her. She knew she was being given a chance to do valuable field research that could be useful not only to the FWP, but also to her own later writings.

Hurston took immediate advantage of her opportunity. No other FWP assignment consumed her more fully. Her copious notes when typed amounted to twenty-six pages. We have no way of knowing exactly what her instructions had been, but her field notes suggest that she had been sent to record "life history" interviews and turpentine expressions for recently planned FWP auxiliary publications.

Hurston's only finished piece became her essay "Turpentine," in which she accompanied black woods rider John McFarlin, "a sort of pencil-shaped brown-stained man in his forties," on his daily ride through the woods as he checked his men's daily tasks. These turpentine woods riders were the backbone of the industry, the straw bosses who oversaw the turpentiner's chipping, dipping, and pulling. They checked and corrected the slashes, looked for unmarked trees, and evaluated progress.

In the essay, Hurston took the role of a curious participant-observer who watched John McFarlin as he made his rounds supervising his men. Through Hurston's curiosity, the reader's interest is piqued. "Talk about knowing his business!" she wrote. "[He] can ride a 'drift' and with a glance tell if every 'face' on every tree has been chipped." Nothing missed her careful observation: the look and feel of the woods, the way in which McFarlin treated his men, as well as his own attitude toward his work. "Turpentine woods is kind of lonesome," McFarlin told Hurston. From McFarlin's description of turpentining she learned specific details about the duties of chippers, dippers, pullers, and woodchoppers, the rate of pay, and how the woods rider evaluated the work of his men.[112]

Hurston's feelings emerge a decade later as she drew from her Cross City experience impressions and information that shaped powerful scenes and characters for *Seraph on the Suwanee*. She weaves her experience riding the woods with foreman McFarlin into the novel, using it as background to describe Jim Meserve's career as a turpentiner. In *Seraph*, she wrote:

> Jim Meserve was what was known as a woodsman in the turpentine plan of things. That meant that he was the resident head of a camp. He ran the commissary and kept the accounts of the workers and made out the time. It was his job to "ride the woods" before the semimonthly payday and evaluate the work of the chippers and dippers. Their pay depended upon the number of trees streaked or dipped. The number of trees could be reduced by the number improperly worked. The limit of a "drift," a territory of one chipper, is known as the "butting-line" or "block," so as Jim rode his horse from drift to drift, he could enjoy both the beauty and the solitude of the pine woods.[113]

While "Turpentine" remains Hurston's only finished Cross City piece, her other interviews, although rough, are filled with vibrant information about the turpentiners' lives. Jim Byrd was a thirty-year veteran of the trade who had worked his way up the turpentine ladder, rising through the industry from the lowliest job of "scraping," cleaning up debris around the trees to prevent fires, to one of the most trustworthy—foreman of a processing still that turned the pine sap into rosin. His testimony offered a candid look at the life of a turpentiner who generally liked his job, despite its low pay. Knowing little else, Byrd saw few of the industry's defects.[114]

Hurston's interviews with Byrd and McFarlin illuminated the lives of the turpentiners, but what of their girlfriends, wives, and lovers? Hurston sought them out in the camp drinking establishment known as a "jook." These jook joints, which were usually nothing more than a one-room shanty with a juke box, a few tables and chairs, and a makeshift bar, were the lifeblood of the camps. In her early field collecting days, Hurston found the drama of many settlements played out in the jooks, where gambling, drinking, and gossip took place.[115]

It was only natural that she sought out a similar establishment in Cross City. This must have been the place where she met Ethyl Robinson, a "jook woman" who made her money selling sexual favors to the turpentiners. Hurston befriended her and stumbled upon the secrets of the camps. Robinson was a good subject to interview, for she saw or heard about everything that went on in the camps. As a jook woman, Robinson boasted she could "scare up as much in a night" as most black women did in a week. She bristled and fumed about the horrible working conditions that women had to bear—about the cook at the local school who made three dollars a week and fed 150 children a day. However, her most most startling revelation dealt not with work, but with camp abuses. Robinson told Hurston tales of beatings and forced marriages. It seems that the supervisor of the camps, a man named George, had recently "beat a woman on [camp] #25 for not helping his [George's] wife." Robinson related, "He come into Cross City and beat another and forced her to return to her husband at #25." She noted that he "beat the husband of the first woman also." Cliff Clark, a resident of Cross City who had worked for the Aycock and Lindsay Company and knew George, readily recalled George's meanness in an interview fifty years later. As supervisor of the camps, George, like Miss Catherine, exercised life-and-death control over the workers. Clark testified that beatings were common. Blacks who refused to work were killed and thrown into the nearby sinkholes. Women who refused to work or return to their husbands were punished in the same manner.[116]

Hurston found that as horrifying as were these conditions, the abuse of women went even deeper and recalled slave days. In Hurston's notes was a reference to the "paramour issue" that Robinson told her "to write up." Clark sheds light on Robinson's reference. He explains that the "paramour issue" referred to the fact that white woods riders could claim the sexual favors of any black woman in the camps they fancied. If the woman's husband dared to protest, he was murdered and his body weighted with cement and thrown into the nearby Gulf of Mexico.[117]

Robinson's revelations had so taken Hurston aback that she had not dared write down their full import. Deeply moved, Hurston confided to Bill Duncan, "There is a terrible situation here." Duncan, Cook, and Hurston wanted to inform Miss Catherine of camp abuses, though it is more than likely that as resident manager she knew of them. The lawlessness of the area is well documented. Not far from Cross City, the once thriving lumber town of Rosewood had once stood. In early January 1920, enraged whites burned the town, killed many of its residents, and drove the rest away. The whites who participated were never punished; no black dared refer to the incident. Atrocities in Cross City nearly two decades later were treated in the same manner. The truth of the matter was that in remote areas of the state, white people could perpetrate violence against blacks with immunity.[118]

Hurston's ability to gain people's confidence had enabled her to penetrate appearances and get to the heart of matters in Cross City. To the area's black residents, she represented a rare sight indeed: a member of their own race who was working for the federal government. She had impressed them that she was *above all* concerned about their lives. No doubt in telling Hurston of these abuses, Robinson believed that, as an outsider and government agent, she could do something to rectify them.[119] After leaving Cross City, Hurston reportedly wrote Catherine Lindsay, but nothing ever came of these disclosures.[120]

Hurston's detailed field notes were never used by the Federal Writers' Project. Yet, Hurston knew their potential value and use for her later work. Years later while writing *Seraph on the Suwannee*, she would draw from her Cross City experience not only information and impressions, but also dialogue recorded for the FWP's *Lexicon of Trade Jargon*. Hurston's "Turpentine Notes—Cross City" contains dozens of expressions used in "signifying" and "playing the dozens." This was a topic the FWP did not address, nor did it have any need for this material in any of its publications. It is evident that Hurston was gathering these expressions for her own later use. She knew that in this ritualized jesting, hidden from most whites, was rooted the rich humor and verbal agility of the people. In the wilds of west Florida's turpentine camps, playing the dozens usually centered around "Saturday night" behavior. Black men played the dozens with jook women or their most intimate friends. "You musta been born in March, but you going to die in July if you don't watch out." Much of it was ribald. The goal was for each player to "top" his rival's more clever reply:

Dirty-Red, I was so glad when I come a man.
Is yo a man?
That's what they say. Little man with big stuff.

In this "ritual of permitted disrespect," as Lawrence Levine describes it, the winner flaunted his verbal facility, originality, ingenuity, and humor.[121]

The privacy of the ritual cannot be overemphasized. Fifty years later, Clifford Clark, who had been a part of this wild, bawdy scene, refused even to discuss playing the dozens with a white woman interviewer and quickly changed the topic of discussion.[122]

Hurston continued to play a central role in the WPA recording expedition as she was called back to Jacksonville in mid-June to help organize the first of two recording sessions. Herbert Halpert, who headed the expedition, was due to arrive in the city with the equipment, carefully stored in a converted World War I ambulance outfitted by workers from the Federal Theater Project. As a young man of twenty, Halpert was just beginning his long career as a folklorist, but had already garnered extensive experience in the field. He was one of the few folklorists with field recording experience. He knew how to transport, repair, and set up the cumbersome equipment as well as to conduct the first-person interviews, an integral part of the recording sessions from which important background information was obtained. Despite frequent breakdowns and a grueling travel schedule, years later Halpert recalled, "The high point of my fieldwork experience came when I traveled the South to record folk songs for the WPA and the Library of Congress."[123]

Hurston organized the black recording session held at the Clara White Mission. The people attending had been tapped either by Hurston directly or by some other FWP worker. From the tape of the session, we hear railroad and dock workers calling out their chants with the rhythmic beat of hammers sounding in the background. A gospel choir led by Annie Whitaker sings "Gotta Make a Hundred, Ninety-nine and a Half Won't Do." As Mrs. Whitaker explained, the song described the perfect effort required of Christians and had come to her years earlier, "right out of the sky, straight from God." She related that it was now sung at African American revivals all over Florida. Eartha White, the city's leading black philanthropist and founder of the Clara White Mission, contributed an old slave tale, "Why Horses Have White Faces." In the accompanying interview she explained that it was a ghost story her slave mother had told her in order to make her behave.[124]

Hurston took center stage in the Jacksonville recording session as she called out orders to the musicians and sang eighteen songs. These included railroad work songs, jook ditties, gambling tunes, and Bahamian folk songs that she had collected in the late 1920s in Florida and in the West Indies. The short interviews conducted by Herbert Halpert before each selection offer rare insight into Hurston's perceptions of her folk collecting and presentations of herself as a folklorist. Even more revealing are the dynamics between herself and Halpert—his noticeably condescending manner and her ever-ready replies.[125]

As the drums beat and singers performed in Florida for the WPA recorder, Congress was beating its own kind of drums to signal the end of federal sponsorship of the WPA arts projects. Conservatives had finally voted down federal sponsorship of the projects and cut back on the WPA relief rolls by implementing the "eighteen-month rule," which terminated any WPA worker who had been on relief for more than eighteen months, as Zora Neale Hurston was about to be. Zora Neale Huston's time on the FWP was over.

Sensing what was to come, as did most FWP employees, Hurston had begun earlier to look for employment. The award of an honorary doctorate in June 1939 from her alma mater, Morgan State, as well as her reputation as a dramatist helped her find an academic position as drama instructor at North Carolina College in Durham.[126]

Hurston's forced departure from the WPA reflects basic changes that were taking place on the national and international scenes. The WPA arts projects had proved beneficial to a host of talented but needy artists and professionals during some of the worst days of the Great Depression, but by 1939, they had become an increasing political liability. World War II loomed, and Roosevelt could not afford to alienate the conservatives in Congress. Although decrying the Dies Committee's tactics, New Dealers chose not to fight to save the FWP. Two months after Congress terminated federal sponsorship of the arts projects, Hitler invaded Poland and World War II began.

Hurston had experienced the most creative phase of the program. Although the FWP did not officially end until the spring of 1943, its real life was over with the end of federal sponsorship. Once it was transferred to state control, as most were, its mission and character were altered as it became an arm of state government churning out bureaucratic publications like agricultural bulletins and instructional pamphlets. Even its name was changed to the Florida Writers' Program.

The sudden loss of federal control affected the future of Hurston's FWP manuscripts. Under the 1939 reorganization, Henry Alsberg was fired. The FWP began closing down its publishing projects. Plans for promising national publications like the *Lexicon of Trade Jargon* and other life history volumes were cast adrift. Once Sterling Brown left the project after 1939, the state was left with little motivation to publish *The Florida Negro*. As a result of these developments, the only portion of Hurston's FWP writings to be published was her guidebook folklore. Thus as Zora Neale Hurston's story so effectively illustrates, the richest cache of FWP materials, documentation about American life that dug more deeply into the national fabric than did the surface description of the guides, remained in the files and was largely forgotten.[127]

Governmental patronage for Hurston had proved far less stressful and demanding than her years as Charlotte Mason's protégée, when her patron had asked for a strict accounting of every penny spent and exercised supervision over her projects. As a federal writer, Hurston had for the most part been able to control her own destiny. Although assigned topics, she wrote what she wanted when she wanted. Unmet deadlines did not provoke major crises.

Most important of all, Hurston had been able to maintain her pride by keeping up appearances. To all but an intimate few, Hurston appeared to be a successful writer living in Eatonville working on her fifth book. She lived comfortably and maintained a lifestyle above the norm, shown by her ability to keep a car, which in the late 1930s was a luxury.

In late June 1939, just before leaving the FWP, Hurston married Albert Price III, a twenty-three-year-old Jacksonville resident. Price worked for the WPA in the recreational division. The couple most likely met at the black WPA project offices housed in the Clara White Mission. Hurston's writings for *The Florida Negro* would have brought her here to consult black project writers' files. Little is known about Price, except for his tender age. One can only speculate on the reasons Hurston chose to marry a man twenty-five years her junior.[128] Her father, John Hurston, had married a young woman twenty-five years his junior following Lucy Hurston's death, and this may have influenced her decision. Or perhaps Hurston was attempting to recreate the romance in *Their Eyes Were Watching God* of Janie and Tea Cake, who were fifteen years apart. Her marriage might also have been triggered by her nieces' leaving her and getting married. (Winifred, like her sister before her, met an Eatonville man and married.)

Hurston derived much from the FWP, but what had the Florida FWP achieved by having a published writer and a trained folklorist of Hurston's caliber on its staff? The Florida unit possessed a rare opportunity indeed, but failed to take advantage of it. It gave Hurston substantive assignments, which she completed, sending in writing of such high literary quality that it needed no editing. Yet it used only a minuscule fraction of her writings in their publications. Considering the size of Florida's automotive guidebook—six hundred pages—her folklore and town histories were a tiny drop in a very large bucket. It is safe to add that if the national office had not pushed so stridently for these guidebook inclusions, summoning her to Washington for the final edit of the state's book, even they might have been deleted.

The Florida FWP's gravest error proved to be its failure to use Hurston's literary talent and anthropological training to shape *The Florida Negro*. Not only did it not give her editorial control, but it deleted her essays from the final manuscript after she left the project. The deletion of Zora Neale Hurston's writings from Florida's African

American manuscript points to weaknesses in the overall program itself. In their attempts to illuminate the nation's African American roots, Henry Alsberg and other New Deal visionaries had conceived a noble dream indeed. Yet the New Deal was first and foremost a political phenomenon. Once political goals had been achieved—once black support for Roosevelt in the 1936 election had been garnered—the dream was cast adrift. Black layoffs in Florida exceeded those of whites in 1937. Whereas ten black writers worked on the *Florida Negro* project in 1936, only two were employed in 1939, Zora Neale Hurston being one of them. Tepid support was given African American studies in the national office; Sterling Brown served only part-time and was gone after 1939. Thus the New Deal's noble dream of hiring black writers like Hurston to highlight the nation's African American roots in the end was subverted by the racism and paternalism of the Jim Crow South. The dream proved far too idealistic for the times.[129]

In the end, the FWP served Hurston and others well. It made her rethink old ideas, sparked new research, and kindled new writing. It proved a strong, sturdy bridge between her early and later careers. Hurston's FWP experience reminds us that despite the program's administrative bungles, relief origins, and untimely death, it enriched and continued to inspire the individual lives it had helped. As Hurston's long-submerged writings prove, it created a vast storehouse of field research and writings.

Zora Neale Hurston attending a national exhibit of Federal Writers'
Project work some time in 1938. Hurston promoted the Project for both
the national and state offices.

One of the main thrusts of Hurston's Cross City trip was to find folklore for the WPA recorders. Robert Cooke took this picture of Cross City turpentiners demonstrating their song and dance.

While in Cross City scouting songs for the WPA's Southeast Recording Expedition, Hurston documented the area's turpentine industry. She rode the woods observing chippers such as this one slashing the pines to extract the sap.

Hurston's interview with Jim Byrd documented in detail the inner workings of a turpentine distillery and described in full the dangers of distilling work. Industrial accidents and injuries were frequent.

Hurston was given ample free time to roam the turpentine camps.
Robert Cooke took this photograph of her relaxing on the porch of
a turpentine shanty.

An unknown photographer captured this photograph circa the late 1930s of Eatonville citrus pickers, like John Hamilton ("Seaboard"), who worked at local groves.

This barn-like structure on the edge of Eatonville resembles "the house by the lake" where Hurston lived while working as a federal writer.

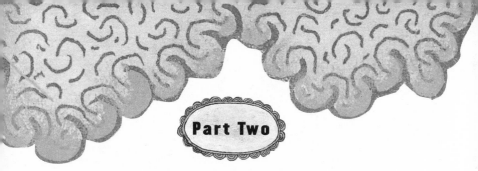

Part Two

Readings

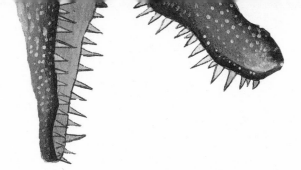

Folklore

Hurston's writings for the WPA's Federal Writers' Project are brimming with her ideas on folklore in general and Florida folklore in particular. Hurston shared common ground with the FWP's folklore program. Indeed the FWP's goals—to illuminate the lives of ordinary folk, people whose hopes, dreams, and daily work remained for the most part undocumented—had long been her own. Both she and her FWP supervisors knew that the people's folklore defined the shape they gave their world, identified their adversaries, outlined their dreams. The folklore that Hurston contributed to the FWP did all of these things and more. The first selection, "Proposed Recording Expedition into the Floridas," identifies and explains the beauty and uniqueness of Florida folklore. Her essay "Go Gator and Muddy the Water" provides a sampler of relevant folklore and explains the people's need to create it. "Other Negro Folklore Influences" compares Floridian and Bahamian music, dance, and humor. "The Sanctified Church" is a sophisticated observer's account of one of the most striking features of African American folk culture. "New Children's Games" analyzes the meaning, derivations, and significance of black children's play. Finally, there are two groupings of Hurston's writings on specific tales and legends, "Negro Mythical Places" and "Other Florida Guidebook Folktales."

Proposed Recording Expedition into the Floridas

After taking the helm of the Federal Writers' Project's folklore program in 1938, Benjamin Botkin called together representatives from various branches of the WPA to create the Joint Committee on Folk Art. As its first venture, the committee planned an expedition to the southeastern United States to record the songs and stories that WPA workers had uncovered.

Botkin was aware of Zora Neale Hurston's knowledge of Florida, and he called upon her to write a report outlining recording possibilities in her state. "Proposed Recording Expedition into the Floridas" was the direct result of that request. Lyrical, analytical, and complete, the report is a masterful synthesis of what Hurston termed "the inner melting pot of the great melting pot America." She divides Florida into four subregions: the tobacco-and-corn-growing area of northwest Florida, the maritime and shipping district of the eastern seaboard, the vegetable-growing lands of central Florida, and the "foreign culture area" of south Florida. In each area Hurston identifies the folkloric influences. A single stanza from a local folk song begins each sectional commentary, imparting as nothing else could the subtle nuances that distinguished the section. The verse heading the description of Area I, west Florida, conveys the lingering racism of the region's plantation roots:

Got my knap-sack on my back
My rifle on my shoulder
Kill me a nigger 'fore Saturday Night
If I have to hunt Floridy over.

She identifies in each subregion the unique economic, social, and cultural factors that shaped its folkloric elements. In every section she suggests unusual people for the recorders to interview, like "Pap" Drummond of Fernandina Beach, who told tales about pirates and buried treasure.

Read critically, this report echoes Hurston's own abiding interest in south Florida's melting pot of "Bahamians, Haitians, African Americans, and American whites," where much of her own folkloric collecting had centered. She invited the WPA recorders to follow in her footsteps.

At the end of each regional summary, Hurston calls attention to elements of black folk religion that could be found in every section of the state. Again she is identifying her own ongoing career interests. A year after leaving the WPA, Hurston traveled to Beaufort, South Carolina, to continue her study of primitive churches. She believed these churches to be one of the richest untapped veins of cultural information still available.

There is perhaps no better example of the WPA's ability to draw from Hurston first-class folkloric commentary than this essay. She offered her own field inquiry and concerns as a springboard for the government's extended research and recordings. Unfortunately, when the WPA recorder did appear, very little of the material that Hurston suggested was recorded. The summary itself has been buried in the Library of Congress for over half a century.

■ ■ ■

⬤➤ Area I

Got my knap-sack on my back
My rifle on my shoulder
Kill me a nigger 'fore Saturday Night
If I have to hunt Floridy over
(Sung by Waldo Wishart, Ocala, Fla.)

West Florida extends from the Perdido River on the west to Lake City on the east, from the Alabama–Georgia state lines on the north to as far south as Gilchrist County on the south. This is the Florida so well known to Spanish-French-English-Indian fighting tradition. The material is plentiful. There are men and women still alive who know and can tell of the struggles of four different groups of people to control this area. There are the Creole songs and customs of Pensacola and surrounding area. There are the African American Negro folk tales in abundance and the religious and secular songs in plenty. This is a sort of culture pocket that is not being drained off so rapidly as other sections of the State.

The reason for this is that this section of Florida is the cotton-corn-tobacco region. Here people live under the patriarchal agrarian system. The old rules of life hold here. Down on the Gulf Coast of this section are large fishing and oyster settlements with their songs and traditions. West Florida is a very rich and little-touched area. It is worth an expedition in itself. In addition to the purely cultural material to be found, it is possible to make recordings that bear on the economic and sociological setup of the area. The new is hurling itself, not so effectually, against the old and feudal life. The interviews should be particularly interesting. The shipyards and the like are the culture beds of other maritime folk creations. A serious study of blank verse in the form of traditional sermons and prayers [could be made].

👁 Area II

De Cap'n can't read, de Cap'n can't write
How does he know that the time is right?
I asked me Cap'n what de time of day
He got mad and throwed his watch away.
(Sung by Willie Joe Roberts, Jacksonville, Fla.)

From the St. Marys River, which is the Georgia–Florida boundary line, to Gainesville on the south and from Lake City to the Atlantic Ocean is northeast Florida.

In this area we have a conglomerate of many cultures. There is the Georgia–Alabama "Cracker" with his farms and cows, his old-English traditions and ways. But here also are the descendants of the great old English, French, and Spanish families and their monuments and culture. And occupation, the matrix of culture creation among peoples, is in this area in a lavish way. In addition to the vast number of songs and the like handed down from England, there is a lavish of the stuff created by both black and white around their works. From Fernandina, Mayport, and St. Augustine there is the lusty material of the sea folk. Jacksonville is a great port with the bustling chanting stevedores and roustabouts. The Jacksonville–Callahan area is full of railroad songs, chants, and stories.

Ah Mobile!
Hauh!
Ah in Alabama
Hauh!
Ah Fort Myers!
Hauh!
Ah in Florida!
Hauh!
Ah let's shake it!
Hauh!
Ah let's break it!
Hauh!
Ah let's shake it!
Hauh!
Ah just a hair!
Hauh!
(Sung by Fred James Watson, 1225 W. Duval St., Jacksonville, Fla.)

In this same area there are men like old "Pap" Drummond of Fernandina who tell tales of the pirates who roamed the Spanish Main and tell of buried treasures. Pap Drummond lives in his shack on the outskirts of Fernandina with his "family" of rattlesnakes rustling now and then in their dugout near at hand, and draws a long bow on the lawless men of the skull and crossbones of yesteryear. He claims to have aided in the last recovery of pirate treasure.

Interviews with the turpentine-timber workers of this area would be extremely interesting. There has seeped in some impulse to change the old for the new, and the comments of the laborers are very interesting from a sociological viewpoint.

There are river men in this area who have plied the St. Johns River for more than one generation with their songs, stories, and observations. Some have seen the last of the Indian fighters go. Look for the roots of traditional sermons and prayers.

👁 Area III

I got a woman, she shake like jelly all over
I got a woman, she shake like jelly all over
Her hips so broad Lawd, Lawd her hips so broad

And they found him, found him in between two mountains
And they found him, found him in between two mountains
With head hung down, Lawd, Lawd with head hung down
(Sung by Richard Jenkins, Mulberry, Fla.)

From the Palatka–Gainesville line south to Tarpon Springs on the west coast and Fort Pierce on the east coast is a section of peninsular Florida devoted to citrus fruits, turpentine, lumber, phosphate, celery, and tourists. This area includes the justly famous Polk County, so full of varied industries that it is full of songs and story. The most robust and lusty songs of road and camp sprout in this area like corn in April. "Uncle Bud," "Planchita," "Ella Wall," and other real characters poured into song and shaped into legend. It would be profitable in this region to make a series of recordings on John, Jack, Big John de Conquer(or), that great hero of Negro folklore who is Brer Rabbit and Brer Rabbit is him.

Look for fine examples of those folk poems in blank verse known as sermons and prayers.

👁 Area IV

Evalina, Evalina, you know the baby don't favor me, eh,
Eh, you know the baby don't favor me.
(Sung by Lias Strawn, Miami, Fla.; drummed by "Stew Beef")

South Florida: This is the foreign culture area of Florida. This foreign culture has not yet [been] absorbed into the general pattern of the locality, or [is] just beginning to make its influence felt in American culture. This foreign area really should be designated as a collection of areas. The sanctified church is strong in this area with its rebirth of spiritual and anthem making.

A. Tarpon Springs—A Greek sponge-fishing area with its Greek Orthodox ceremonies and other folk songs and customs.

B. Tampa—With the largest Latin colony in the United States. Here the Cuban songs, dances, and folk ways color the soil and flavor the air.

C. Miami—A polyglot of Caribbean and South American cultures.

> 1. More than 30,000 Bahamians with their songs, dances and stories, and instrumentation.
> 2. Haitian songs, dances, instrumentation, and celebrations.
> 3. American Negro songs, games, and dances.
> 4. American white songs and stories.
> 5. African songs, dances, and instrumentation. There is a pure African colony there.

D. Everglades—Raw, teeming life of the frontiers and mining or construction camp type. A hot mixture of all the types of material of the area. Worth the whole trip alone. The life histories, social, ethnic studies would be rare and vital.

E. Key West to Palm Beach—Bahamian and Cuban elements in abundance. Also the ranch settlement at Riviera. All new to study and worth a great deal of investigation.

Summary

There is not a state in the Union with as much to record in a musical, folklore, social-ethnic way as Florida has. To be sure California has the Chinese, Japanese, Filipino population which Florida lacks, but these Asiatic cultures seem so far from our own that they don't enter the stream of American culture at all. No other state in the Union has had the history of races blended and contending. Nowhere else is there such a variety of materials. Florida is still a frontier with its varying elements still unassimilated. There is still an opportunity to observe the wombs of folk culture still heavy with life. Recordings in florida will be like backtracking a large part of the United States, Europe, and Africa, for these elements have been attracted here and brought a gift to Florida culture each in its own way. The drums throb: Africa by way of Cuba; Africa by way of the British West Indies; Africa by way of Haiti and Martinique; Africa by way of Central and South America. Old Spain speaks through many interpreters. Old England speaks through black, white, and intermediate lips. Florida, the inner melting pot of the great melting pot America.

(Sanctified Anthem)

O Lord, O Lord
Let the words of my mouth, O Lord
Let the words of my mouth, meditations of my heart
Be accepted in Thy sight, O Lord
(Sung by Mrs. Orrie Jones, Palm Beach, Fla.)

Go Gator and
Muddy the Water

This essay was Hurston's third and final draft of the folklore and music chapter for *The Florida Negro*. It provides a veritable treasury of Florida folklore and is one of Hurston's most complete discussions of the origin of folklore. Her essay departs from the simple narrative style of *Mules and Men*, as it offers a creative analysis of folklore's development and the people's need to create it.

"Go Gator" opens with the development of song and moves on to the progression of prose, concluding with folk tales showcasing the gallery of black heroes and tricksters. She presents tales of the slave trickster John, powerful "Big John de Conquer," and the newly discovered Florida prison hero "Daddy Mention." These hero tales, Hurston believed, served as success stories that "all weak people create to compensate for their weakness."

Hurston's inclusion of the "Daddy Mention" tales demonstrates the wide collecting net of the FWP folklore program. These were the work of black federal writer Martin Richardson, who visited the "Blue Jay," one of Florida's largest prisons that housed the state's more trustworthy inmates. Here he interviewed Bob Davis, who was a "frequent inmate," Frank White, who was serving "his second time," and "Panama Red" Hooper, who was working off a six-month sentence. These men related to Richardson the "Daddy Mention" tales. Amused by their candid telling, Richardson wrote in his field notes: "When or where 'Daddy Mention' came into being will require some research; none of the 'guests' at the 'Blue Jay' seems to know. Only one thing is certain about the wonder-working gentleman: he must have existed, because so many people claim to have known him."[1]

Hurston was impressed with the tales as a prime example of the hero cycle unfolding. Using the editorial license afforded her in compiling "Go Gator," she included them as well as some of Richardson's commentary about them.

As Hurston herself recognized, the tales are important in their ability to highlight the prisoners' feelings about their captivity. Daddy Mention's frequent and clever escapes, his defiance of the racial mores of the day, and his never-ending quest for freedom mirrored the antics and heroics of John, Jack, or Big John de Conquer. More than anything else, a close reading of the tales conveys the inmates' feelings about the harsh racial realities of the Florida prison system in the 1930s.

■ ■ ■

Folklore is the boiled-down juice of human living. It does not belong to any special time, place, nor people. No country is so primitive that it has no lore, and no country has yet become so civilized that no folklore is being made within its boundaries.

Folklore in Florida is still in the making. Folk tunes, tales, and characters are still emerging from the lush glades of primitive imagination before they can be finally drained by formal education and mechanical inventions.

A new folk hero has come to be in the Florida prison camps and his name is Daddy Mention. It is evident that he is another incarnation of Big John de Conquer, that hero of slavery days who could outsmart Ole Massa, God, and the Devil. He is the wish-fulfillment projection. The wily Big John compensated for the helplessness of the slave in the hands of the masters, and Daddy Mention does the same for the convict in the prison camp.

In folklore, as in everything else that people create, the world is a great big old serving platter, and all the local places are like eating plates. Whatever is on the plate comes out of the platter, but each plate has a flavor of its own because the people take the universal stuff and season it to suit themselves on the plate. And this local flavor is what is known as originality. So when we speak of Florida folklore, we are talking about that Florida flavor that the story and song makers have given to the great mass of material that has accumulated in this sort of culture delta. And Florida is lush in material because the state attracts such a variety of workers to its industries.

Thinking of the beginnings of things in a general way, it could be said that folklore is the first thing that man makes out of the natural laws that he finds around him—beyond the necessity of making a living. After all, culture and discovery are forced marches on the near and the obvious. The group mind uses up a great part of its life span tying to ask infinity some questions about what is going on around its doorstep. And the more that the group knows about its own doorstep, the more it can bend and control what it sees there, the more civilized we say it is. For what we call civilization is an accumulation of recognitions and regulations of the commonplace. How many natural laws of the things have been recognized, classified, and utilized by these people? That is the question that is being asked in reality when the "progress" of a locality is being studied. Every generation or so some individual with extra-keen perception grasps something of the obvious about us and hitches the human race forward slightly by a new "law." For instance, millions of things had been falling on and about men for thousands of years before the falling apple hit Newton on the head and made him see the attraction of the earth for all unsupported objects heavier than air. So we have the law of gravity.

In the same way, art is a discovery in itself. Seen in detail it is a series of discoveries, perhaps intended in the first instance to stave off boredom. In a long-range view, art is the setting up of monuments to the ordinary things about us, in moment and time. Examples are the great number of representations of men and women in wood and stone at the moment of the kill or at the bath; or a still moment of a man or beast in the prime of strength, or a woman at the blow of her beauty. Perhaps the monument is made in words and tune, but anyway, such is the urge of art. Folklore is the art of the people before they find out that there is any such thing as art, and they make it out of whatever they find at hand.

Way back there when Hell wasn't no bigger than Maitland, man found out something about the laws of sound. He had found out something before he even stood erect to think. He found out that sound could be assembled and manipulated and that such a collection of sound forms could become as definite and concrete as a war-ax or a food tool. So he had language and song. Perhaps by some happy accident he found out about percussion sounds and spacing the intervals for tempo and rhythm. Anyway, it is evident that the sound arts were the first inventions and that music and literature grew from the same root. Somewhere songs for sound-singing branched off from songs for storytelling until we arrive at prose.

The singing grew like this. First a singing word or syllable repeated over and over like frogs in a pond; then followed sung phrases and chanted sentences as more and more words were needed to portray the action of the battle, the chase, or the dance. Then man began to sing of his feelings or moods, as well as his actions, and it was found that the simple lyre was adequate to walk with the words expressing moods. The Negro blues songs, of which Florida has many fine examples, belong in the lyric class; that is, feelings set to strings. The oldest and most typical form of Negro blues is a line stating the mood of the singer repeated three times. The stress and variation is carried by the tune and the whole thing walks with rhythm. Look at the "East Coast Blues" and see how:

Love ain't nothing but the *easygoing* heart disease;
Love ain't nothing but the easygoing heart *disease;*
Oh, *love* ain't nothing but the *easygoing heart disease.*

The next step going up is still a three-line stanza. The second line is a repetition of the first so far as the words go, but the third line is a "flip" line that rhymes with the others. The sample that follows is from a widespread blues song that originated in Palm Beach:

When you see me coming h'ist your window high;
When you see me coming h'ist your window high;
Done got bloodthirsty, don't care how I die.

Incidentally, this is the best-known form as far as the commercial blues are concerned because in the early days of the commercial blues,

Porter Grainger, who wrote most of these songs, followed this pattern exclusively.

The blues song "Halimuhfask" is still more complicated as to word pattern. The title is a corruption of Halifax. The extra syllables are added for the sake of rhythm:

You may leave and go to Halimuhfask,
but my slow drag will-uh bring you back;
Well, you may go, but this will bring you back.

Progress in construction is even more evident in "Angeline." Here is seen a pattern of a stanza of a rhymed couplet which also rhymes with the succeeding couplet. In addition, it carries out connected thought.

Oh, Angeline! Oh, Angeline!
Oh, Angeline that great, great gal of mine!
And when she walk, and when she walk
And when she walk, she rocks and reel behind!
You feel her legs, you feel her legs,
You feel her legs, and you want to feel her thighs;
You feel her thighs, you feel her thighs
You feel her thighs, then you want to go on high;
You go on high, you go on high,
You go on high, then you fade away and die!
Oh, Angeline! Oh, Angeline!
Oh, Angeline that great, great gal of mine!

"Uncle Bud," that best-loved of Negro working songs, is a rhymed couplet with a swinging refrain:

Uncle Bud is a man, a man in full;
His back is strong like a Jersey bull.
REFRAIN: Uncle Bud, Uncle Bud, Uncle Bud, Uncle Bud, Uncle Bud
'Taint no use in raising sand.
You got to take that scrap of Grandpa's land.
REFRAIN
Uncle Bud's got cotton ain't got no squares
Uncle Bud's got gal ain't got no hairs.

Folk song making has become rather well developed when it arrives at the stage of the ballad. "Delia," from around Fernandina, and "John Henry," from who knows where, are good examples.

Delia

Coonie told Delia on a Christmas Eve night,
If you tell me 'bout my mama I'm sho going to take your life.
She's dead, she's dead and gone.

(Coonie shoots Delia to death in several verses)

Coonie in the jailhouse drinking out a silver cup
Poor Delia in the graveyard don't care if she never wake up
She's dead, she's dead and gone.

(Coonie justifies his killing of Delia)

Mama, oh, mama, how could I stand
When all round my bedside was full of married men
So she's dead, she's dead and gone.

John Henry

John Henry driving on the right-hand side,
Steam drill driving on the left,
Says before I'll let your steam drill beat me down,
I'll hammer my fool self to death, lawd!
Hammer me fool self to death.

John Henry told his captain,
Says when you go to town,
Please bring me back a nine-pound hammer,
And I'll drive your steel on down, lawd!

John Henry went upon the mountain
Just to whip a little steel,
But the rocks so tall, John Henry so small,
He laid down his hammer and he cried, lawd!
He laid down his hammer and he cried.

John Henry had a little woman,
The dress she wore was red,
Says I'm going down the track and she never looked back
I'm going where John Henry fell dead, lawd!
Going where John Henry fell dead.

A ballad catches the interest of everybody in that it is more or less a story that is sung. The power of the group to create and transmit a story is increased. Before, there was music mostly for music's sake. But in the ballad the storyteller is merely using the vehicle of music to carry a tale. The interest of the listener has shifted from sound and rhythm to characterization and action. The music has become the servant of the words. Looping back to the more primitive forms, it is evident that the often meaningless words are mere excuses for repeating the haunting tune. But in the ballad the words make the tune. Take "John Henry," for example, and it is plain that the words and the music are one and the same thing. Read the words aloud and you have the tune. The stresses and lack of stresses all come where they would naturally be if the story were told without music. In other words, the ballad is the prelude to prose.

The ballad is, however, not the only road to prose. Among the other progressions are the folk rhymes. In biology it is generally accepted that the evolution of an organism is reviewed in the embryo. In folk literature it is the same. Anyone who has been around children knows that they pass through various phases from the mere repeating of pleasing single notes to the phase of rhyme-making. This usually occurs when they are six and eight years old. These verses seldom make sense. They are made for the sake of sound. The child is discovering sound laws for himself. The adult primitive does the same thing on his way to prose. So, rhyme for the sake of sound furnishes evidence of the youth of literature. The second step is a combination of sound and sense. Every nation and race has a large body of observations on life coupled with rhyme for the sake of sound. Here are some samples from the Florida area:

1.

Love is a funny thing, love is a blossom;
If you want your finger bit, poke it at a possum.

2.

Counting from your little finger back to your thumb;
If you start anything I got you some.

3.

Nought is a nought, figger's a figger;
All for the white man, none for the nigger.

4.

Some love collards, some love kale;
I love a girl with a short shirt tail.

5.

The wind may blow, the door may slam;
That what you shooting ain't worth a damn.

In each of these rhymes there is a sense line and a sound line. The speaker might easily have said what was necessary without the rhyme, but it was felt that the couplet was more forceful and beautiful than the simple statement. But the real significance of these rhymes is that there is no thought of vocal or instrumental accompaniment—just a talking sentence. So, that brings it right next door to prose.

Folk Tales

The age of prose in every locality and among all races overlaps the twilight of poetry. Like song, prose grows from the short and often pointless tale to the long and complicated story with a smashing climax. All this is quite evident in the folk tales of the Negro American. A single incident, or even a vivid description, is often offered as a story. Here are some samples of this from various parts of Florida:

1.

Once there was a man and he was so little that he had to climb up on a box to look over a grain of sand.

2.

It was a man and he was so big and fat till he went to whip his little boy for something. The little boy run up under his papa's belly and hid under there for six months.

3.

(A common way of telling a story is to dramatize it)

Storyteller: What is the ugliest man you ever seen?

Helper: Oh, I seen a man so ugly that he could set up behind a jimson weed and hatch monkeys.

Another Helper: Oh, that man wasn't so ugly! I knowed a man that could set up behind a tombstone and hatch hants.

Storyteller: Aw, them wasn't no ugly men you all is talking about! Fact is, them is pretty mens. I knowed a man and he was so ugly that you throw him in the Mississippi River and skim ugly for six months.

4.

(Explanation of the hurricane of 1925)

So the storm met the hurricane in Palm Beach and they set down and ate breakfast together. Then the hurricane said to the storm, "Let's go down to Miami and shake that thing!"

5.

They have strong winds on the Florida west coast, too. One day the wind blowed so hard till it blowed a well out of the ground. Then one day it blowed so hard till it blowed a crooked road straight. Another time it blowed and blowed and scattered the days of the week so bad till Sunday didn't come until late Tuesday evening.

6.

It gets pretty hot around Tampa, too. Two mens got on the train at Jacksonville to go to Tampa and they was wearing blue serge suits. The weather got so hot till when the train got to Tampa just two blue suits stepped down off the train. The mens had done melted out of the suits.

7.

They raises big vegetables down around the Everglades, too. Yes, sir! That's rich land around down in there. Take for instance, my old man planted sweet potatoes one year and when it come time to dig them potatoes, one of them had done got so big till they had to make a sawmill job out of it. Well, they built a sawmill and put whole crews to work cutting up that big old sweet potato. And so that year everybody in Florida had houses made out of sweet potato slabs. And what you reckon everybody ate that year? Well, they lived off of potato pone, made out of the sawdust from that great big old tater my old man raised.

8.

Round Ocala you can find some land that is sort of poor for raising things. My old man bought some land over round there and it was so poor till he give it to a congregation to build a church. Well, they called a preacher and built the church, and they all met there to open it up. But that land was so poor till they had to telegraph to Jacksonville for ten sacks of commercial (fertilizer) and spread it on the ground so they could raise a tune.

9.

My old man was late planting his corn that year. Everybody else had corn knee-high. So one morning my old man took and told us we better plant some corn. So my brother John was opening the furrows and I was dropping corn and my baby brother was coming long behind me hilling it up. So I looked back over my shoulder and seen that the corn was coming right up behind me as fast as I was dropping it and it was growing so fast till I knowed that it wasn't going to make nothing but fodder. So I hollered to my baby brother Joel to sit down on some of them hills of corn to stunt the corn so it would make corn instead of fodder. Well, my brother Joel done like I told him and the next day he dropped us back a note and said, "Passed through heaven yesterday at twelve o'clock selling roasting ears to the angels."

10.

Sis Snail took sick in the bed, you know, and she didn't get no better so after while she hollered for her husband and she told him say, "Honey, I reckon you better go get the doctor for me. I'm *so* sick and don't look like I'm on the mend." Brer snail told her, "All right, I'll go get the doctor for you. Give me time to go get my hat." So Sis Snail rolled from pillar to post in the bed. After seven years she heard a noise at the door and she said, "I know that's my husband with the doctor, and I am so glad! Lord knows I'm so sick. Honey, is that you with the doctor?" Brer Snail hollered back and told her, "Don't try to rush me! I ain't gone yet." It had took him seven years to get to the door.

11.

It was close to Christmastime, so God was going to Palatka. The Devil was walking the same road and he seen God and jumped behind a stump to keep God from seeing him. He done that for two reasons. In the first place he wanted to catch God's Christmas gift and get a present out of God and then again he didn't want to give God nothing, so that's how come he jumped behind the stump. God was sort of busy in His mind counting over His new angels so He wasn't paying no attention to stumps. When He got right along there, the Devil jumped out from behind the stump and hollered, "Christmas gift!" at God. God seen what the Devil had done but He kept right on walking. He just look back over His shoulder and said, "Take the East Coast." And that is why people have so many storms and mosquitoes on the East Coast because it is the Devil's property.

Big John de Conquer

(Big John de Conquer is the culture hero of the American Negro folk tales. He is Jason, or Ulysses, of the Greeks; Baldur of the Horse tales; Jack the Giant Killer of European mythology. He is the story that all weak people create to compensate for their weakness. He is a projection of the poor and humble into the realms of the mighty. By cunning or by brute might he overcomes the ruling and utterly confounds its strength. He is among men what Brer Rabbit is among the animals. In the Ole Massa tales he compensates the slave for his futility. He even outwits the Devil, who in Negro mythology is smarter than God.)

Ole Massa had a nigger named John, you know. Ole Massa lakted [liked] John because he learned everything Ole Massa tried to teach him and he never forgot nothing you told him. Ole Big John used to go and stand in the chimney corner every night at the big house and listen to see what Ole Massa talked about. Then he would go back and tell the other niggers in the quarters that he could tell fortunes. If he hear Ole Massa tell Ole Miss that he was going to kill hogs next day, John would come back and tell them, "Well, Ole Massa is going to kill hogs tomorrow." Them others would ask, "What make you say that, John?" "I'm a fortune-teller and nothing ain't hid from me." So sure enough when Ole Massa come out next morning he would tell everybody to get ready for the big hog killing. It kept on like that until they all believed John when he said anything.

The way he fooled Ole Massa and Ole Miss was he was hanging round the back door when he seen the water throwed out that Ole Miss had done bathed in and he seen her diamond ring get throwed out in the water. John seen a turkey gobbler grab up that ring and swallow it down. So when Ole Miss looked for her ring and couldn't find it she started to cry and say that somebody had done stole her diamond ring that Ole Massa give her for a birthday present. John, he come told Ole Massa that he could find the ring for Ole Miss. So Massa told him to find it if he could and he would give John a fine shoat. So John told him to kill that certain turkey gobbler and he would find the ring. Ole Massa told him not to fool him into killing his prize turkey rooster, do he aimed to kill Ole John. When he killed the gobbler there was the ring sure enough, so then Ole Massa believed everything John told him.

One day when Ole Massa was talking with some more betting white folks he told them, "I got a nigger that can tell fortunes." One man told him, "No, he can't tell no fortunes neither!" Massa told him, "I'll bet you forty acres of bottomland that Big John can tell fortunes." The man told Ole Massa, "Why don't you back your judgment with your money? Bet me something! I'll bet you my whole plantation that nigger can't tell no fortunes. I'll bet you every inch of land I own."

Ole Massa had him where he wanted him, so he reared back and said, "I didn't know you was going to make a betting thing out my statement, but since I see you do, let's make it worth my time. I'm a fighting dog, you know, and my hide is worth money. I bet you my whole plantation against yours, and every horse and every mule and every hog and every nigger on the place, that my nigger John *can* tell fortunes." So they took paper and signed up the bet. They made arrangements to prove the thing out a week from that day. Massa come on home and told John what he had done, and he told John, too.

"John, I done bet everything I got in the world on you and you better not make me lose everything I got, do I sure will kill you."

The day of the bet come and Ole Massa told John the night before to be ready bright and soon to go to the betting ground with him to prove out the thing. Ole Massa used to ride a fine prancing horse, and John used to ride a fat mule right along with Massa everywhere he went. He used to be up every morning and have Massa's saddle horse at the door before Massa get out of bed. But this morning Massa was up and had done saddled his own horse and had to go wake John up. John was so scared because he knowed he couldn't tell no fortunes and he knowed that he was going to make Ole Massa lose everything he had and then Massa was going to shoot him. So he hung way back behind Massa on the way to where they was holding the bet.

When they got to the place, why, everybody was there from all over the world because they had done heard about this big bet. John and Ole Massa got there and Ole Massa lit down from his horse real spry, but John just sort of slid off of that mule and stood there. The man that was betting against Ole Massa had the privilege to fix the proof, so John was carried off a little piece and when he come back he seen a great big old iron wash pot turned down over something and the man told John to tell them what was under that wash pot. Ole Massa told him he better think good 'cause he sure meant to kill him if he didn't tell it right and made him lose his place. It was very still because all of them there had seen what was under the pot except John, and they was all waiting to hear what he had to say. John looked at the pot and he walked all around it three or four times but he couldn't get the least inkling of what was under that pot. He begin to sweat and to scratch his head and Ole Massa looked at John and he begin to sweat, too. Finally John decided he might just as well give up and let Ole Massa kill him and be done with it. So he said, "Well, you got the old 'coon at last." When he said that, Ole Massa throwed his hat up in the air and let out a whoop. Everybody whooped except the man that was betting against Massa, because that was what was under the pot, a big old 'coon (raccoon). So none of them never did know that John didn't know what was under that pot. Massa give John his freedom and a hundred dollars, and Massa went off to Philadelphia to celebrate and left John in charge of everything.

When Massa went off to celebrate his bet, he left John in charge of everything. So soon as him and Ole Miss got on the train to go, John sent word round to all the plantations to ask his friends to a big eating and drinking. "Massa is gone to Philly-mah-york (corruption of New York and Philadelphia) and won't be back in three weeks. He done left everything in my charge. Come on over for a big time." He sent word round to all the niggers on all the plantations like that. While some of them was gone to carry out the invitations, he told some more to go into Massa's lot and kill hogs until you could walk on them.

So that night everybody come to eat and drink and John really had done spread a table. Everybody that could get hold of the white folks' clothes had them on that night. John, he opened up the whole house and took Ole Massa's big rocking chair and put it upon Massa's big bed, then he got up in it to sit down so he could be sitting high when he called the figures for the dance. He was sitting up in his high seat with a box of Massa's fine cigars under his arm and one in his mouth: "Ladies right! First couple to the floor! Sashay all!" When he seen a couple of poor-looking white folks come in, John looked at them and said, "Take them poor folks out of here and carry them back to the kitchen where they belong. Give them plenty to eat, but don't allow them back up front again. Nothing but quality up here."

You see, John didn't know that was Ole Massa and Ole Miss done slipped back to see what he would do in their absence. So they ate some of the good meat first and then they washed the dirt off their faces and come back into the room where John was sitting up in the rocking chair in the bed.

"John," Massa told him, "now you done smoked up my fine cigars and killed up my hogs and got all these niggers in my house carrying on like they crazy when I trusted you with my place. Now I am going to take you out to that big old persimmon tree and kill you. You needs a good hanging and that is just what you are going to get."

John asked him, "Massa, will you grant me one little favor before you kill me?" Massa told him yes, but hurry up because he was anxious to hang a man who would cut the capers that John had cut. John called his friend Ike to one side and told him, "Ike, Ole Massa is going to take me out to the persimmon tree to hang me. I want you to go get up that tree with a box of matches and every time I ask God for a sign, you strike a match. That is the only way to save my life." So Ike run ahead and got up the tree with the box of matches. After while here comes Massa with John and a rope to hang him. He throwed the rope over a high limb and tied one end around John's neck. At that time John said, "Massa, will you let me pray before you kill me?" Massa told him to go ahead and pray, but he better pray fast because he was tired of waiting to hang him. So John got down and said, "O Lord, if you mean to stop Massa from hanging me, give me a sign." When he said that Ike struck a match, and when Massa see that light up the trees, he begin to get scared. John made out he didn't see Massa flinch and he kept right on praying. "O Lord, if you mean to kill Ole Massa tonight, give me another sign." Ike struck another match. Ole Massa said, "That's all right, John, don't pray no more." John kept right on praying. "O Lord, if you mean to put Massa to death tonight with his wife and all his chillun, give me another sign." Ike struck a whole heap of matches at that and Ole Massa lit out from there, running just as fast as he could. And after that he give John and everybody else they freedom and that is how Negroes got their freedom—because John fooled Ole Massa so bad.

(There are numerous other stories of John's doings with Ole Massa, of his tricking strong men out of contests, of his visits to Heaven and Hell, and of his victories over the Devil. Casual listeners have confused John de Conquer with John Henry, but this is far from correct. John Henry is celebrated for one single act of bravery and strength, in the manner of Casey Jones, while John de Conquer is a hero cycle yet unfinished. The strongest herb used in hoodoo is called Big John de Conquer root. Nothing is supposed to stand against it. There have been no stories of John's death, except the ones told in order to show him carrying on in Heaven. He is up to his old tricks there, also.)

Daddy Mention

Just when or where Daddy Mention came into being, none of the guests at the Duval County (Florida) Blue Jay (prison farm) seem to know. Only one thing is certain about this wonder-working prisoner: every other prisoner claims to have known him.

Not that any of his former friends can describe Daddy Mention to you, or even tell you very many close details about him. They agree, however, that he has been an inmate of various and sundry Florida jails, prison camps, and road farms for years.

In fact, it is this unusual power of omnipresence that first arouses the suspicions of the listener: was Daddy Mention perhaps a legendary figure? Prisoners will insist that he was in the Bartow jail on a ninety-day sentence, "straight up," when they were doing time there. Then another will contradict and say it must have been some other time, because that was the period when Daddy was in Marion County, "making a bit in the road gang." The vehemence with which both sides argue would seem to prove that Daddy was in neither place, and that very likely he was nowhere.

Daddy Mention's Escape   Daddy Mention liked the Polk County jails all right, all except the little jug outside of Lakeland. He told 'em when they put him in there that he didn't think he could stay with them too long.

They had locked him up for vagrancy, you see. And Daddy Mention didn't think much of that, because just like he had told them he had been picking oranges, and just had too much money to work for a week or two. He tried to tell them that he would go back to work as soon as he got broke, but you know you can't say much in Polk County.

So they locked Daddy Mention up; gave him ninety straight up.

(Ninety days with no time off for good behavior.) He went on the stump-grubbing gang. Soon he got to the Farm.

It was afternoon when Daddy Mention started to work, and he made the first day all right. He fussed a little, kind of under his breath, when he saw what the prisoners et for supper, but he didn't say much. Then next morning he et breakfast—grits and bacon grease, but no bacon—with the rest of us, and went out to the woods.

Before it was ten o'clock—you know you start at six in Polk County—Cap'm Smith had cussed at Daddy two or three times; he didn't work fast enough to suit 'em down there. When he went for dinner he was growlin' at the table: "Dey ain't treatin' me right."

After dinner, when we lined up to go back to the woods, Cap'm Smith walked over to Daddy. "Boy," he hollered, "you gonna work this afternoon, or you want to go to the box?"

Daddy Mention didn't say nothing at first, then kinda slow he said: "Whatever you want me to do, Cap'm."

Cap'm Smith didn't know what to make of that, and he put Daddy in the box in a hurry. He didn't go back for him that day, neither. He didn't go back till the next day. "You think you want to come out of there and work, boy?" he asked Daddy Mention, an' Daddy Mention told him again: "Whatever you want me to do, Cap'm."

I didn't see Cap'm Smith then, but they tell me that he got so hot you could fry eggs on him. He slammed the box shut, and didn't go back for Daddy Mention for another day.

Daddy Mention didn't get out then, though. Every day Cap'm Smith asked him the same thing, and every day Daddy Mention said the same thing.

Finally Cap'm Smith figured that maybe Daddy Mention wasn't trying to be smart, but was just dumb that way. So one day he let Daddy Mention out, and let him go with another gang, the tree-chopping gang, working just ahead of us.

Daddy Mention was glad to get out, 'cause he had made up his mind to go Tampa. He told some of his gang about it when the Cap'm wasn't listening. But Daddy Mention knew that he couldn't run away, though; you can't do that down there. They'd have you back in jail before you got as far as Mulberry.

Oh, no! Daddy Mention knew he had to have a better plan. And he made one up too. None of us knew much about it, 'cause he didn't talk about it then. But we begin seein' him doing more work than anybody else in his gang; he would chop a tree by hisself, and wouldn't take but one more man to help him lift it to the pile. Then one day, when he was sure his Cap'm saw him, he lifted one all by hisself and carried it a long ways before he put it down.

The Cap'm didn't believe any man could grab one of them big pines and lift it by hisself, much less carry it around. He call Daddy Mention and make him do it again, then he make him do it so the other guards kin see it.

It wa'nt long before the Cap'm and his friends was picking up a little side money betting other folks that Daddy Mention could pick up any tree they could cut. And they didn't fuss so much when he made a couple of bumpers (nickels) showing off his lifting hisself.

So it got to be a regular sight to see Daddy Mention walking around the jail yard carrying a big tree in his arms. Everybody was getting used to it by then. That was just what Daddy Mention wanted. One afternoon we came in from the woods, and Daddy Mention was bringing a tree-butt with him. The Cap'm thought one of the other guards musta told him to bring it in, and didn't ask him nothing about it.

Daddy Mention took his tree-butt to the dining room and stood it up by the wall, then went on with the rest of us and et his dinner. He didn't seem in no hurry or nothing, but he just didn't have much to say.

After dinner he waited till nearly everybody got finished, then he got up and went back to his log. Most of the Cap'ms an' guards was around the yard then, and all of 'em watched while Daddy Mention picked up that big log.

Daddy Mention clowned around in front of the guards for a minute, then started towards the gate with the log on his shoulder. None of the guards didn't bother him, 'cause who ever saw a man trying to escape with a pine butt on his shoulder?

You know you have to pass the guard's quarters before you get to the gate in the Lakeland Blue Jay. But Daddy Mention didn't even turn around when he pass, and nobody didn't say nothing to him. The guards musta thought the other guards sent him somewhere with the log, or was making a bet or something.

Right on out the gate Daddy Mention went, and onto the road that goes to Hillsborough County. He still had the log on his shoulder. I never saw him again till a long time after, in Tampa. I never did figure out how he got into Hillsborough County from Polk, with watchers all along the road, after he left the Lakeland Blue Jay. So I ask him.

He say, "I didn't had no trouble. I jes' keep that log on my shoulder, and everybody I pass thought it had fell off a truck, an' I was carrying it back. They knew nobody wouldn' have nerve enough to steal a good pine log like that and walk along with it. They didn't even bother me when I got out of Polk County. But soon's I got to Plant City, though, I took my log to a little woodyard an' sold it. Then I had enough money to *ride* to Tampa. They ain't gonna catch me in Polk County no more."

Daddy Mention and the Mule   Daddy Mention git a long trip to Raiford once. Dey wuz a lot of people workin' on de Canal near Ocala, an' dey wuz makin' good money. Daddy Mention, he wuz makin' better money dan dey wuz, though. You see, he wa'nt workin' 'xackly on de Canal; he wuz sellin' a little whiskey on de side to dem dat wuz.

Dey didn't let the Ocala police arres' nobody on de Canal. De county cops didn' bother you much, neither. Dere wuz some special men could bother you, but ef you didn' raise a ruckus, dey wouldn' care.

But Daddy Mention uster have to go to Ocala whenever his liquor run out. He wuz smaht, though; he uster git one of de white men on de camp t' drive him in an' bring him back. Dat-a-way de police in Ocala didn't had a chance t' git him.

It uster make de cops mad as a stunned gopher to see Daddy Mention come ridin' right into town wid dis here white feller, den go ridin' back to de Canal again, an' dey couldn' git dere han's on him.

But one time Daddy Mention done jes git his little load o' likker an' dey had started back when de white feller he see somebody he knowed. So he git out o' de truck an' tole Daddy Mention to wait a minute.

He didn' have to tell him dat; de cop come an' put Daddy Mention where he kin wait a long time, real comfortable. De policeman he wait a long time for a chance to lock Daddy Mention up. So he think he would have a li'l fun wid him. So he started pretendin' to joke with Daddy Mention, an' kiddin' him about allus ridin' into town wid dat white man: "You mus' t'ink you as good as white folks," he told Daddy Mention, an' laugh.

Daddy Mention he think de cop wuz really playin' wid him, so he started tellin' stories. He tole him 'bout how de Lord wuz makin' men, an' put all de dough in de oven. "He take out de fust dough," say Daddy, "an' it wa'nt nowhere near brown; it wuz jes yaller. So He set it aside, an' later it become all dem folks what lives in foreign countries, dem Turks an' all. Den He take out a real brown batch of dough." Daddy Mention tole de policeman how dis batch look well-done an' season' jes right. "Dese wuz de cullud folks," say Daddy. De policemans dey all laugh; Daddy didn't see dem winkin' at each other.

"What become of de rest of de dough?" dey ask Daddy. "Oh, dat," say Daddy, "dat what wuz lef' over, dey done make all de policemans in de world outa dat." Den Daddy Mention he laugh as hard as he could, an' de policemans dey laugh too.

I don' know ef de jedge done laugh, though. He give Daddy Mention two years de nex' day. Dat's how Daddy git to Raiford an' git to know Jinny.

It take Daddy Mention a long time to figure out he really in de Big Rock for two years or better. When he finally git it through his haid, he begin tellin' folks he wouldn' stay dere no two year.

You can' beat Cap'm Chapman Jinny, dey try tell him. But Daddy Mention he laugh; he ax 'em how, ef he done drown houn' dogs in de swamp an' done dodge guards wid double-barrel Winches' kin a mule stop him?

Lotsa other prisoners dey try to tell Daddy Mention, but he wouldn' have it no other way but he mus' try to escape an' make it to de Okeeno-kee Swamp up de other side o' Olustee.

So one mornin', soon as dey let us out in de yard, Daddy Mention ups an' runs. He wuz in good shape, too; he beat dem shotguns a mile.

When he git a chance to look back over his shoulder he see one o' de guards put his finger in his mouth and whistle. But didn' no dog come; out come trottin' a li'l, short, jackass-lookin' mule, an' she back into a li'l drop-bottom cart wid nobody techin' her.

It don' take but a minute to hitch dat Jinny into dat cart, an' by de time de harness wuz on her all of de dogs wuz in de bottom of de cart an' it was flyin' down de fiel' after Daddy Mention.

Daddy Mention wuz smaht; he had stole one o' de other prisoners' shoes befo' he lef', so when he git to de woods he take off his shoes an' put on dese. Den he throw his shoes in de ditch, to fool de dogs. An' it done fool 'em, too. Daddy he had time to fin' hisself a good big oak tree an' kivver hisself in it befo' de dogs come an' lost his trail. So he wuz doin' a lot of laughin' to hisself when dey went on across de ditch an' kep' on barkin' an' runnin' furder away. De cart that Jinny wuz pullin de dogs in wuz standin' a li'l ways off fum his tree too.

Daddy Mention he wuz busy watchin' de dogs and figurin' when could he come down and hit it fer de swamp, when he feel somepin grab at his pants. Befo' he kin figure out what it is, it had tore de whole seat out of 'em, an' maybe a li'l bit of Daddy Mention too. Den he see it wuz Jinny. She have two feets on de bottom of de tree an' wuz reachin' for another piece of Daddy Mention's pants. He try to hurry up a li'l higher, an' one of his feets slip down a li'l. Dat when Jinny show him she et leather too.

Daddy, he didn' know what to do. He go round to de other side o' de tree, an' jump down to run. Jinny she come right on behin' him. He have to keep goin' dat same way, 'cause de dogs wuz still runnin' roun' de other way.

Befo' Daddy knowed it Jinny had done chase him right back to de prison fence. But he think even gittin' back inside'd be better'n git et up by dat wil' mule, so he lit out fer de top o' de fence. Den jes as he git almos' over, Jinny bit again. Dis time dere wa'nt no pants for her to bite, so she jes grabbed a mouthful o' Daddy Mention.

An' dat's where he be when Cap'm Chapman come; right dere, wid a good part o' him in Jinny's mouth. It wuz a long time befo' he kin sit down to eat. Dat don' worry him so much, 'cause in de box where he wuz you don' eat much, anyway.

Other Negro Folklore Influences

Hurston originally included this comparison of Floridian and Bahamian folklore, music, and humor in the second draft of her folklore and music essay, the piece that in final form became "Go Gator and Muddy the Water." As she expanded that essay, she made "Other Negro Folklore Influences" into a separate piece.

"Other Negro Folklore Influences" complements and extends Hurston's earlier fieldwork done in south Florida and in the Bahamas in the late 1920s. She drew on that work for "Dance Songs and Tales from the Bahamas," which she published in the *Journal of American Folklore* in 1930. From these dances she created "The Great Day," her folkloric production first performed off-Broadway in 1932, and many times after that in such places as the New School for Social Research in New York and various Florida locations between 1932 and 1939.

This essay reflects Hurston's long experience and deep anthropological grounding. In it she links African American and Bahamian cultures with their African past, making her one of the first folklorists, along with Melville Herskovits, to do so.

■ ■ ■

On the west coast, from Key West to Tampa, there is a tremendous addition of Cuban music, tales, and folkways. On the east coast, from Fort Pierce to Key West, there is an even stronger element seeping into Negro folkways. This is something brought into the United States by the flood of Negro workers from the Bahamas. The Bahamian music is more dynamic and compelling than that of the American Negro, and the dance movements are more arresting; perhaps because the Bahamian offerings are more savage. The Bahamian, and the West Indian Negro generally, has had much less contact with the white man than the American Negro. As a result, speech, music, dancing, and other modes of expression are infinitely nearer the African. Thus the seeker finds valuable elements long lost to the American Negro. This is because the Negro slave on the continent of North America, unlike the island slave, was never allowed to remain in tribal groups. This was both to prevent uprising and to speed up his Americanization. Also, on American soil the slave came into direct contact with the master and the master's family almost daily, whereas the system of absentee ownership was prevalent in the West Indies, and the slave owner might not visit his plantations once in ten years. There might be three hundred slaves under the care of one white overseer, who could not concern himself with the personal contact that most masters relish with their own property.

Bahamian drum rhythms are truly magnificent. The songs are nearly all dance songs and the words are mere excuses to introduce the tunes. A rhythmic phrase is repeated until the fire-tuned drum grows cold and slack in the head and must be tuned and tightened by fire again. Then another tune is introduced.

Of the dance tunes, there are two main types: the jumping dance and the ring dance. The jumping dance tune is short and repetitious. As soon as a dancer chooses a partner, it begins all over again. The length varies. There are "one move" rhythms, two moves, and so on. For instance, in a three-move dance, the dancer "cuts pork"; enters the circle and does a solo dance; chooses a partner and retires.

Lime, Oh, Lime

Lime, Oh, Lime, (cutting pork, a preliminary movement) Juice and all;
Lime, Oh, Lime, Dessa hold your back (Leaps into ring);
Oh, Dessa! (one move) Oh Dessa! (two moves)
Oh Dessa! etc.

The ring play is more elaborate and florid, though it is actually less difficult to do. The dancer chosen enters the ring at the first syllable of the verse and moves around the ring in search of a partner. All dancers in the ring clap their hands loudly throughout the movement. The selected partner steps out of the ring when a rhythmic moment arrives.

Bone Fish

Good morning, Father Fisher, good morning, Father Brown;
Have you any sea-crabs, sell me one or two
Bone fish is biting, have no bait to catch him;
Every married man got his own bone fish.

(The circling ceases and the dancer faces his choice.)
Eh, ah, looy loo!
(This continues until original dancer leaves the ring so that the other may in turn choose a partner. Then, the verse begins all over again.)

One is astonished to find that all of the Bahamian tunes have an African tribal origin. Let the dancers but hear an air and they can instantly tell you to which tribe it belongs. This is a Nango, that an Ibo, another a Congo, another a Youraba (the proudest and most arrogant of all the Negro tribes in the West Indies). One hears such screams of outrage—"What! A Congo man stand in the fact of a Youraba and talks such! Don't you cheek me, Congo!"

Nightly in Palm Beach, Fort Pierce, Miami, Key West, and other cities of the Florida east coast the hot drumheads throb and the African-Bahamian folk arts seep into the soil of America.

Also in Florida are the Cuban-African and the Bahamian-African folk tales. It is interesting to note that the same Brer Rabbit tales of the American Negro are told by these islanders. One also finds the identical tales in Haiti and the British West Indies. Since it is not possible for these same stories to have risen in America and become so widely distributed through the western world wherever the Negro exists, the wide distribution denotes a common origin in West Africa. It has been noted by Carita Doggett Corse that these same tales are told by the

Florida Indians. But this does not mean that they are purely Indian tales as those recorded by John R. Swanton (*Myths and Tales of the Southeastern Indians*, Bulletin 88, Bureau of American Ethnology, Smithsonian Institution). On the contrary, it merely accentuates the amount of contact which Negroes have had with Southeastern Indians in the past. Since it is well known that runaway slaves fled to the Indian communities of southern Georgia and Florida in great numbers, the explanation of the Brer Rabbit tales among the Indians is obvious.

One fact stands out as one examines the Negro folk tales which have come to Florida from various sources. There is no such thing as a Negro tale which lacks point. Each tale brims over with humor. The Negro is determined to laugh even if he has to laugh at his own expense. By the same token, he spares nobody else. His world is dissolved in laughter. His "bossman," his woman, his preacher, his jailer, his God, and himself, all must be baptized in the stream of laughter. A case in point is the explanation of why Negroes are black:

"You know God didn't make people all of a sudden. He made them by degrees when He had some spare time from the creating He was doing. First start off He took a great big hunk of clay and stomped it all out until it was nice and smooth. Then He cut out all the human shapes and stood them up against His long gold fence to dry. Then when they was all dried, He blowed the breath of life into them and they walked on off. That had took God two or three working days to do that. Then one day He told everybody to come up and get their eyes. So they all come and got eyes. Another day when He had some spare time He called everybody to come up and get their noses and mouths, and they all come got them. Then one day He give out toenails and so on till people was almost finished. Then the last thing He called everybody and told them, 'Tomorrow morning at seven o'clock I am going to give out color. I want everybody here on time because I got plenty creating to do tomorrow and I don't want to lose no time.'

"Next morning at seven o'clock God was sitting on His high throne with His high gold crown on. He looked north, He looked west, He looked east, and He looked Australia; and blazing worlds was falling off His teeth. There was the great multitude standing there before Him. He begin to give out color right away. He looked at a great big multitude over at His left hand and said, 'Youse yellow folks.' They said, 'Thank you, Massa,' and walked off. He looked at another squaddle and told them, 'Youse red people.' They thanked Him and went off. He told the next crowd, say, 'Youse white people.' They said, 'Thank you, Jesus,' and they went on off. God looked around on His other hand and told Gabriel, 'Look like I miss some multitudes.' Gabriel looked all around the throne and said, 'Yes sir, it is some multitudes missing. I reckon they will be along after while.' So God set there a whole hour and a half without doing a thing. After that He said, 'Look here, Gabriel, you go and find them multitudes that ain't got their color yet and you tell them I say they better come on here and get their color because when I get up from here today I am never to give out no more color. And if they don't hurry and come on here pretty soon they won't get none now.'

"Gabriel went off and way after while he found great multitudes that didn't have no color. Gabriel told them they better come on up there and get their color before God changed His mind. He was getting mighty tired of waiting. So they all jumped up from where they was and went running on up to the throne hollering about 'Give us our color! We want our color! We got just as much right to have some color as anybody else!'

"The first one that got to the throne couldn't stop because those behind kept on pushing and shoving until the throne was careening way over one side and God got vexed and hollered, 'Get back! Get back!' But they misunderstood Him and thought He said 'Get black,' so they just got black, and we been keeping the thing up ever since."

This will to humor and building to a climax which is so universal in the American Negro tales is sadly lacking in Negro tales elsewhere. This proves that what has always been thought of as native Negro humor is in fact something native to American soil. But anyway, if the other elements that go to fill up the Florida plate of Negro folklore do not possess the humor of the native American Negro, still their contributions certainly are important in other ways, so that Florida has the most tempting, the most highly flavored Negro plate around the American platter.

Biddy, biddy bend, my story is end.
Turn loose the rooster and hold the hen.

The Sanctified Church

First published in the anthology bearing its name,[2] this essay was written for inclusion in the religion chapter of *The Florida Negro*. However, shortly after Hurston left the project, white editors cut the piece from the final draft of the manuscript. This greatly diminished the book, for Hurston was one of the first anthropologists to recognize in the sanctified churches the clearest reflection of African American folk culture.

In its praise and illumination of black folk religion, "The Sanctified Church" continues themes that Hurston expressed earlier in *Jonah's Gourd Vine* (1934) and in "Spirituals and Neo-Spirituals" (1934).[3] In all of these writings, she focuses on continuities between Africa, the slave experience, and African American religion. Through each time period, primitive blacks retained the powerful symbol of the drum, engaged in call-and-response actions, and enshrined their worship in dance and song. Hurston points out the implications of the song, dance, and oratory of these primitive churches and compares them to the staider worship found in "Negro Protestant congregations." Her findings offer compelling commentary on what she believed to be the genius of primitive religion, song-making. The primitive songs, resisted for a time by the more conservative, Protestant congregations, in the end, through their popularity, became mainstream and permeated the life of the very same worshipers who had resisted them. It is in these songs that one finds the clearest expression of the thoughts, feelings, and attitudes of the folk.

Hurston attaches "The White Man's Prayer" to the end of the essay to drive home the point that once blacks became more prosperous and joined mainstream Protestant denominations, African American religious expression lost its vibrancy and feeling. This meant sacrificing the heart of African American culture.[4]

■ ■ ■

The rise of the various groups of "saints" in America in the last twenty years is not the appearance of a new religion as has been reported. It is in fact the older forms of Negro religious expression asserting themselves against the new. Frequently they are confused with the white "protest Protestantism" known as Holy Rollers. There are Negro Holy Rollers, but they are very sparse compared to the other forms of sanctification. The two branches of the sanctified church are (a) Church of God in Christ, (b) Saints of God in Christ. There is very little difference between the two except for the matter of administration.

The sanctified church is a protest against the highbrow tendency of Negro Protestant congregations as the Negroes gain more education and wealth. It is understandable that they take on the religious attitude of the white man, which is as a rule so staid and restrained that it seems unbearably dull to the more primitive Negro, who associates the rhythm of sound and motion with religion. In fact, the Negro has not been Christianized as extensively as is generally believed. The great masses are still standing before their pagan altars and calling old gods by a new name. As evidence of this, note the drumlike rhythm of *all* Negro spirituals. All Negro-made church music is dance-possible. The mode and the mood of the concert artists who do Negro spirituals is absolutely foreign to the Negro churches. It is a conservatory concept that has nothing to do with the actual rendition in the congregations who make the songs. They are twisted in concert from their barbaric rhythms into Gregorian chants and apocryphal appendages to Bach and Brahms. But go into the church and see the priest before the altar chanting his barbaric thunder-poem before the altar with the audience behaving something like a Greek chorus in that they "pick him up" on every telling point and emphasize it. That is called "bearing him up" and it is not done just any old way. The chant that breaks out from time to time must grow out of what has been said and done. "Whatever point he come out on, honey, you bear him up on it," Mama Jane told the writer. So that the service is really drama with music. And since music without motion is unnatural among Negroes, there is always something that approaches dancing—in fact, *is* dancing—in such a ceremony. So the congregation is restored to its primitive altars under the new name of Christ. Then there is the expression known as "shouting," which is nothing more than a continuation of the African "possession" by the gods. The gods possess the body of the worshiper and he or she is supposed to know nothing of their actions until the god decamps. This is still prevalent in most Negro Protestant churches and is universal in the sanctified churches. They protest against the more highbrow churches' efforts to stop it. It must also be noted that the sermon in these churches is not the set thing that it is in other Protestant churches. It is loose and formless and is in reality merely a framework upon which to hang more songs. Every opportunity to introduce a new rhythm is eagerly seized upon. The whole movement of the sanctified church is a rebirth of song-making! It has brought in a new era of spiritual-making.

These songs by their very beauty cross over from the little storefronts and the like occupied by the "saints" to the larger and more fashionable congregations and from there to the great world. These more conscious churchgoers, despising these humble tune-makers as they do, always resist these songs as long as possible, but finally succumb to their charm. So that it is ridiculous to say that the spirituals are the Negro's "sorrow songs." For just as many are being made in this post-slavery period as ever were made in slavery as far as anyone can find. At any rate the people who are now making spirituals are the same as those who made them in the past and not the self-conscious propagandists that our latter-day pity men would have us believe. They sang sorrowful phrases then as they do now because they sounded well and not because of the thought content.

Examples of new spirituals that have become widely known:

1. He Is a Lion of the House of David
2. Stand by Me

3. This Little Light I Got

4. I Want Two Wings

5. I'm Going Home on the Morning Train

6. I'm Your Child

There are some crude anthems made also among these singers:

O Lord, O Lord
O Lord, O Lord
Let the words of my mouth, O Lord
Let the words of my mouth, meditations of my heart,
Be accepted in thy sight, O Lord.
> **(From Psalm 19)**

Beloved, beloved, now are we the sons of God
And it doth not yet appear what we shall be
But we know, but we know
When He shall appear, when He shall appear
We shall be like Him, we shall be like Him
We shall see Him as He is.
> **(From St. Paul)**

The saints, or the sanctified church, is a revitalizing element in Negro music and religion. It is putting back into Negro religion those elements which were brought over from Africa and grafted onto Christianity as soon as the Negro came in contact with it, but which are being rooted out as the American Negro approaches white concepts. The people who make up the sanctified groups, while admiring the white brother in many ways, think him ridiculous in church. They feel that the white man is too cut and dried and businesslike to be of much use in a service. There is a well-distributed folk tale depicting a white man praying in church that never fails to bring roars of laughter when it is told. The writer first found the story in Polk County, but later found it all over the South.

The White Man's Prayer

It had been a long dry spell and everybody had done worried about the crops so they thought they better hold a prayer meeting about it and ask God for some rain. So they asked Brother John to send up the prayer because everybody said that he was really a good man if there was one in the country. So Brother John got down on his knees in the meeting and begin to pray, and this is how he prayed:

"O Lahd"—this pronunciation is always stressed and always brings a laugh—"the first thing I want you to understand is that this is a white man talking to you. This ain't no nigger whooping and hollering for something and then don't know what to do with it after he gits it. This is a white man talking to you and I want you to pay me some attention. Now in the first place, Lahd, we would like a little rain. It's been powerful dry round here and we needs rain mighty bad. But don't come in now with no storm like you did last year. Come cam [calm] and gentle and water our crops. And now another thing, Lahd, don't let these niggers be as sassy this coming year as they have in the past. That's all, Lahd. Amen."

The real, singing Negro derides the Negro who adopts the white man's religious ways in the same manner. They say of that type of preacher, "Why he don't preach at all. He just lectures." And the way they say that it sounds like horse-stealing. "Why, he sound like a white man preaching." There is great respect for the white man as a lawgiver, banker, builder, and the like, but the folk Negroes do not crave his religion at all. They are not angry about it. They merely pity him because it is generally held that he just can't do any better that way. But the Negro who imitates the whites come in for spitting scorn. So they let him have his big solemn church all to himself while they go on making their songs and music and dance motions to go along with it and shooting new life into American music. I say American music because it has long been established that tunes from the street and the church change places often. So they go on unknowing, influencing American music, and enjoying themselves hugely while doing so in spite of the derision from the outside.

New Children's Games

By the late 1930s, the most innovative folklorists were collecting and studying children's play tunes. Abbot Ferris, who got his start as a folklorist on the Mississippi FWP, collected and scouted such tunes for recording by the WPA Joint Committee on Folk Art. In Florida, Hurston joined in the search. Her interest in them dates back to her collecting for *Mules and Men*. With "New Children's Games," Hurston provides commentary missing in this earlier fieldwork.

■ ■ ■

It has been observed that the grown folks' work is the children's play. In the children's games that are widespread over the United States, we find the rhymes of Old England dominating the field. It has been found that these rhymes date mostly from the sixteenth and seventeenth centuries and were the political cartoons of their day. Those verses were the commentaries on British Government out of the mouths of the people.

London Bridge is falling down, falling down, falling down,
London Bridge is falling down, Ah fair lady!

This often-played game of British-American children is now nothing but a bit of tuneful doggerel, but once was a comment on stirring political doings. The final verse:

To the gallows he must go, he must go, he must go,
To the gallows he must go, Ah fair lady!"

This rhyme is said to have come out of the arrest and trial of Charles Stuart, known to history as Charles I of England.

Little Sally Walker, sitting in a saucer
Crying and weeping for, Oh, she has done!
Rise, Sally, rise! Wipe your weeping eyes.
Turn to the East, Sally, Turn to the West,
Turn to the very one that you love the best.

This is said to center around Queen Elizabeth and her unintentional execution of the Earl of Essex, whom she was said to love dearly.

Anyway, we see the grown-ups' serious activities becoming the children's play. The same thing holds true in the Negro children's games. All through Negro life and creation is evident the will to rhythm and it is the thing of Negro children's games. From the Florida east coast comes a sample of almost pure rhythm. There is no movement, none except what little is indicated by the words and the well-timed swinging of the joined hands of the children making up the ring.

Bama, bama, look at Miss Claudia (name of whoever is in the ring at the
    moment) yonder
Miss Claudia picking her bama
Stoop to the corner, stoop,
Stoop to the corner, stoop.
    (With the arms swinging in time, all partly stoop.)
Bama, bama, look at Miss Claudia yonder
Miss Claudia picking her bama
Squat to the corner, squat! Squat to the corner, squat!
Bama, bama, look at Miss Claudia yonder
Miss Claudia's picking her bama,
Rise to the corner, rise! Rise to the corner, rise!
    (Another player is chosen, and so on)

Aunt Dinah's Dead is played for the sake of the hot timing which is so characteristic of Negro folk music in addition to the dance innovations. It is relatively new and from what can be found up to now, seems to have originated in central Florida. It is played to terrific hand-clapping.

PLAYER IN CENTER: Aunt Dinah's dead!
How did she die?
Oh, she died like this!
 (Executes a dance step until the center has exhausted all the dance
 steps he or she knows. Then the next phase begins.)
CENTER: *(Despite the fact that Aunt Dinah's death has been announced*
 several times and the manner of her taking off has been
 demonstrated thoroughly)
Oh, she's living in the country
And she's living in town
And she shakes, shakes, shakes from her hand on down.

Blue Bird

 (Native to Polk County)
Blue bird, blue bird, through my window
Blue bird, blue bird, through my window
Blue bird, blue bird, through my window
Oh, honey I'm tired.
 (The person in the ring is going in and out under the arms of the
 other players.)
Catch a little blue bird pat him on the shoulder
Catch a little blue bird pat him on the shoulder
Catch a little blue bird pat him on the shoulder
 (Suit action to word. Players turn and face each other, two and two,
 and pat shoulders rhythmically.)
Oh, honey I'm tired.

Following the adult Negro pattern of the world well lost for rhythm, it is found that in nearly all cases the Negro handling of the traditional white games has been to step up the time and in other ways to marry them to rhythm. Here is what happened to "Little Sally Walker" in Polk County:

Little Sally Walker
Sitting in a saucer
Rise Sally, *rise!* (Dynamic hand-clapping begins)
Wipe your weeping *eyes!*
Shake it to the *East,* Sally
Shake it to the West, Sally
Shake it to the one that you love the best. *(Hot, hot hand-clapping,*
**   *dancing, and "breaking")***

Let it be said here that the hips under little skirts and britches are really shaken east, west, north, south, and otherwise.

Sissy in de Barn

This game has a very wide distribution and is most popular in Florida. A boy or girl is chosen to be number one in the center of the ring and the circling begins:

Sissy in de barn, join de wedding
Prettiest little gal I ever did see
**   *(Here a partner is chosen)***
Oh, bye and bye, honey arms around me
Say lil Sissy won't you marry me.
**   *(Duet dancing begins here accompanied by hand-clapping)***
Get back gal, don't you come near me
All them sassy words you say,
**   *(Dancing flourish)***
Oh bye and bye, honey arms around me
Say little Sissy won't you marry me.

The most widely distributed play-game among American Negroes is Chick-Mah-Chick-Mah-Craney-Crow. This game has been found in every Negro community in the South, and a variation of it is just as popular in the West Indies. Dr. Melville Herskovits found a version of it in West Africa and also the ceremony of which the American game is a perversion.

Chick-Mah-Chick-Mah-Craney-Crow

One large child is selected to be the crow. He or she squats on the ground with a small stick in his hand with which he marks the "time." Another large child, a girl, is chosen to be the hen immediately behind her, clasping the hen's clothes so that she will be able to keep her (or his) place. The next-smallest child follows and so on until the tiniest little "biddy" is attached to the end of the line. So much for the setup. Now for the action.

The hen, followed by her line of biddies, starts chanting and marching around the squatting crow. All the biddies chant too.

HEN AND CHICKS:
Chick-mah-chick-mah-craney-crow
Went to the well to wash my toe
When I got back my chick was gone
What time, old witch?
CROW: *(Makes mark with stick)* **One!**

The marching and chanting is supposed to keep up until every chick is counted, but actually it seldom goes past three, even when sixteen–twenty chicks are present. The counting over, the crow arises and attempts to catch all of the chicks; the mother hen tries to protect them. The crow flaps his wings and hops rhythmically from side to side. Hen does the same to protect her young. The crow thrusts, tries sudden darts, but the hen parries just as skillfully. Nevertheless, the biddies are finally caught.

CROW: Chickie!
HEN: My chickens sleep!
CROW: Chickie!
HEN: My chickens sleep!
CROW: I shall have a chick!
HEN: You shan't have a chick.
CROW: My pot's a-boiling.
HEN: Let it boil!
CROW: My mama's sick.
HEN: Let her die!

CROW: *(Fainting)* I'm going home.
HEN: There's the road.
CROW: I'm coming back!
HEN: Don't care if you do.
CROW: Oh I shall have a chick!

This keeps up until all of the biddies are caught. Then the crow has them kneeling down with two little sticks atop their heads. He is the host and invites the hen to dinner. She tastes each one of the biddies and in each case declares that they taste like hens.

CROW: Come in and have some dinner, Sis Hen!
HEN: Thanks, Sir. Believe I will have a mouthful with you.
CROW: Taste some of this little brown pullet right here. Sure is good.
    (Hen tastes and smacks lips elaborately)
HEN: Taste just like my little brown pullet I lost yesterday.
CROW: *(Indignantly)* Oh, no, that ain't your little brown biddy nothing of
    the kind!
HEN: Oh yes it is!
CROW: Naw, it ain't, neither!
HEN: Oh yes it is, too. Let's see who she crow for.
*(The child is struck lightly in the back by the crow but she refuses to
    make a sound. The hen strikes her and she crows.)*
Unh hunh, I knowed that was my little pullet.

And so on until the end. Some chicks, if pinched hard enough, can be induced to crow involuntarily for the crow. When the last biddy has declared himself, the hen, without warning, becomes a landed gentleman with hounds and horses. The crow comes to his gate to ask a drink of water and is discovered to be a fox. So the former hen sicks the dog on the fox and they finally run him down and eat him up.

With his love of acting and his extraordinary mimicry, the young Negro has invented some games that are purely mimicry of animals and people. At Eau Gallie, on the Florida east coast, one small boy was observed on his all fours going through the pantomime of a cat defecating, digging a hole, and burying it. Widespread through Florida is the Rabbit

Dance, also done on all fours. The players chant and execute steps with both hands and feet in imitation of the rabbit:

At night time, at the right time
I've always understood
It's the habit of the rabbit
To dance in the wood.

The games that Negro children in Florida play fall in three classes: (1) Purely white games that have been learned by Negro children by contact with whites such as "London Bridge Is Falling Down," (2) White games that have been modified by Negro use, like "Little Sally Walker," (3) Purely Negro games like "Bama," "Rabbit Dance," and "Chick-Mah-Chick." All of them are characterized by the drum rhythms but have been kept alive in America by hand-clapping in the absence of the African drums. They follow the Negro adult interests as the games of the white children follow the white.

Down by the river I heard a mighty racket
Nothing but a bull frog, pulling off his jacket.

Negro Mythical Places

This group of four tales is credited to Florida's turpentiners, who were among the South's most deprived laborers. Turpentiners were for the most part employees of large commercial concerns that utilized a variety of methods (most notably credit at the company commissaries, which charged exorbitant prices for daily necessities) to keep them in constant debt. State laws barring workers from leaving their jobs until their debts were paid meant that most were locked into their posts for life. Some chose flight in the middle of the night, which was a risky business at best. If caught, the employee faced imprisonment.[5]

In a world stacked against them, it is easy to see how turpentiners' folklore provided not only entertainment, but deep psychological release as well. Their whimsical tales offer wry commentary on human foibles, natural happenings, and worldly events and demonstrate that the harder the life, the more imaginative the folklore. One can readily picture these men sitting after hours on the steps of a shotgun house or the porch of some shanty jook joint or club entertaining and lifting each other up as each storyteller tried to outdo his rival. Although these turpentiners were, for the most part, uneducated, the richness of their oral literature illustrates their keen perception and imaginative way of looking at their lives, their loves, and their world.

■ ■ ■ ■ ■ ■ ■ ■ ■ ■ ■ ■

Diddy-Wah-Diddy

"Diddy-Wah-Diddy" provides a clear example of how folklore offered psychological release by helping rural blacks survive poverty in the midst of the Great Depression. In Diddy-Wah-Diddy, workers did not have to concern themselves with making a living, eating, or even cooking. Everything was provided for them. This tale does not appear in any of Hurston's earlier writings. We know from her field notes that she collected it in northern Florida, but she does not say when. Of the story, Hurston wrote, "On Route #17 north of Jacksonville, the white owner of a large barbecue stand has named his place Diddy-Wah-Diddy. He said he did it because he was always hearing the Negroes around there talking about this mythical place of good things to eat, especially the barbecue. So he thought that it would prove a good title."[6]

■ ■ ■

This is the largest and best known of the Negro mythical places. Its geography is that it is "way off somewhere." It is reached by a road that curves so much that a mule pulling a wagonload of fodder can eat off the back of the wagon as he goes. It is a place of no work and no worry for man and beast. A very restful place where even the curbstones are good sitting-chairs. The food is even already cooked. If a traveler gets hungry all he needs to do is to sit down on the curbstone and wait and soon he will hear something hollering "Eat me!" "Eat me!" "Eat me!" and a big baked chicken will come along with a knife and fork stuck in its sides. He can eat all he wants and let the chicken go and it will go on to the next one that needs something to eat. By that time a big deep sweet potato pie is pushing and shoving to get in front of the traveler with a knife all stuck up in the middle of it so he just cuts a piece off of the end and so on until he finishes his snack. Nobody can ever eat it all up. No matter how much you eat it grows just that much faster. It is said, "Everybody would live in Diddy-Wah-Diddy if it wasn't so hard to find and so hard to get to after you even know the way." Everything is on a large scale there. Even the dogs can stand flat-footed and lick crumbs off heaven's tables. The biggest man there is known as Moon-Regulator because he reaches up and starts and stops it at his convenience. That is why there are some dark nights when the moon does not shine at all. He did not feel like putting it out that night.

Zar

In keeping with the theme of being mythical, Zar might be the most elusive place of all. Few persons have ever been there; even fewer have returned.

■ ■ ■

This is the farthest known point of the imagination. It is away on the other side of Far. Little is known about the doing of the people of Zar because only one or two have ever found their way back.

Beluthahatchee

This third mythical place, Beluthahatchee, is a land of forgiveness, where all strident discord is dismissed forever. The Florida guide produced the only published version of this captivating and imaginative tale. White editors refined Hurston's field copy. The version below is the tale just as Hurston wrote it.

Stetson Kennedy, who got his start as a writer and folklorist on the Florida FWP, was so taken with the tale's message that he named his writer's retreat in Green Cove Springs, Florida, "Beluthahatchee."

■ ■ ■

This is country where all unpleasant doings and sayings are forgotten. It is a land of forgiveness. When a woman throws up to her man something that happened in the past (some act that he has perpetrated against happiness), he may merely reply, "I thought that was in Beluthahatchee." (I thought that was forgiven and forgotten long ago.) Under other circumstances one person may say to another, "Oh, that's in Beluthahatchee." (That is already forgotten. Don't mention it. I hold nothing against you.) This place is "the sea of forgetfulness where nothing may rise to accuse me in this world, nor condemn me in the judgment."

Heaven

Like the other mythical places, Heaven follows the theme of being far off and inconveniently out of reach. The story line flows from the drama of an impetuous would-be angel who arrives in Heaven but refuses to follow the rules and wait for his flying lessons. His impatience leads to his eventual demise and quick exit.

On the surface the devilishness of this would-be angel is amusing. It fits the 1930s stereotypes of blacks as being silly or childish. But the tale's meaning goes deeper. One foolish soul had ruined other blacks' chances of ever getting into Heaven. Told in a communal setting, the story invited listeners' comments about the would-be angel's impatience and impertinence. Thus it gave cautionary advice to the younger generation: "Even Heaven belongs to the white man. Follow his rules."[7]

■ ■ ■

In this city there is the celebrated Sea of Glass where the angels go out to glide every afternoon for their pleasure. There are many golden streets, but the two main arteries of travel are Amen Street, running north and south, which is intersected right in front of the Throne by Hallelujah Avenue, running from the east side of Heaven to the west. All of the streets are a pleasure to walk on, but Hallelujah Avenue and Amen Street are "tuned" streets. They play tunes when they are walked upon. They do not play any particular or set tunes. They play whatever tunes the feet of the walker play as he struts. All of the shoes have songs in them too. Everybody's shoes sing sol me, sol do, sol me, sol do, as they walk up and down in Heaven. The rumor is that there are no more Negroes in Heaven. God used to let them go there in great numbers, but one Negro came there who could not wait until Old Gabriel showed him how to fly. He was so eager to use his new wings that he took off over Heaven and got so cocky he tried to fly across God's nose. He fell and tore down a lot of God's big gold and jeweled hanging lamps and knocked over several of those big golded-up vases that are standing all over Heaven. When he got through falling down and breaking up, God just gave him a look and Gabriel knew just what to do. He went to the Negro and ripped off his wings. He told the destruction-maker, "And it will be a long, long time before you get any more wings too." The Negro told Gabriel, "I don't care if I never get no more. I sure was a flying fool when I had 'em." So since that time they have been mighty careful up there and some folks say that no more Negroes have qualified as yet.

West Hell

This tale continues the theme of mythical places, but unlike "Diddy-Wah-Diddy," "Beluthahatchie," and "Heaven," which speak of places of which one dreams, where life is better, "West Hell" is unalluring. The story's characters, Big John de Conquer and the Devil, are more forceful, its plot is more dramatic, and its encoded messages are subtler. The tale highlights the power and conquest of Big John de Conquer, who figures in the essay "Go Gator and Muddy the Water." Hurston developed this character more fully a few years later in her article "High John de Conqueror," published in *The American Mercury* (1943).[8] Although reminiscent of the adventurer Jack in *Mules and Men*, Big John proves to be a more dramatic and leading character. He bears the name of the most potent root in hoodoo to symbolize his superhuman strength. He possesses all the characteristics of the admired hero—wit, speed, and luck, as well as superb skill at fighting. Above all, Big John de Conquer could outwit the Devil, who symbolized the white man, by taking his most prized possession, his daughter. Hurston's "West Hell" voices a theme commonly found in African American lore: the triumph of the less powerful trickster over his stronger adversary.

Since guidebook space was at a premium, only an abridged version of the tale appeared. Below is the original version of the tale, just as Hurston submitted it.

■ ■ ■

West Hell is the hottest and toughest part of that warm territory. The most desperate malefactors are the only ones condemned to West Hell, which is some miles west of Regular Hell. These souls are changed to rubber coffins so that they go bouncing through Regular Hell and on to their destination without having to be carried by attendants, as the

Devil does not like to send his imps into West Hell oftener than is absolutely necessary. This suburb of Hell is celebrated as the spot where the Devil and Big John de Conqueror had their famous fight. Big John de Conqueror had flown to Hell on the back of an eagle, had met the Devil's daughters and fallen in love with the baby girl child. She agreed to elope with him and they had stolen the Devil's famous pair of horses that went by the name of Hallowed-Be-Thy-Name and Thy-Kingdom-Come. When the Devil found out about it, he hitched up his equally famous jumping bull and went in pursuit. He overtook the fleeing lovers in West Hell and they fought all over the place, so good a man, so good a Devil! But way after while John tore off one of the Devil's arms and beat him, and married the Devil's daughter. But before he left Hell he passed out ice water to everybody in there. If you don't believe he done it, just go down to Hell and ask anybody there and they will tell you all about it. He even turned the damper down in some parts of Hell so it's a whole lot cooler there now than it used to be. They even have to make a fire in the fireplace in the parlor now on cool nights in the wintertime. John did that because he says him and his wife expect to go home to see her folks sometime and he don't like the house kept so hot like the Devil has been keeping it. And if he go back there and find that damper has been moved up again he means to tear up the whole job and turn West Hell into an icehouse.

Other Florida Guidebook Folktales

Like the five previous tales, the four that follow are linked to common themes. They offer African American explanations of Florida's natural phenomena, such as the weather, the fertility of the soil, and animal names. They often end with a wry twist on human behavior.

■ ■ ■ ■ ■ ■ ■ ■ ■ ■ ■ ■

Jack and the Beanstalk

The African American version of this well-known tale appeared in the Florida guidebook as part of the automotive tour leading through the state's phenomenally rich muck lands surrounding Lake Okeechobee in south-central Florida. Hurston knew the area well. She had collected there and set her most memorable scenes in *Their Eyes Were Watching God* there. In that work, she describes the place as having "dirt roads so rich and black that a half mile of it would fertilize a Kansas wheat field."[9] The story illustrates the soil's fertility. A longer version of it appears in the essay "Go Gator and Muddy the Water."

■ ■ ■

Two brothers were planting corn. Just as soon as the first brother popped the seed into the hole, it sprouted immediately, growing to maturity before the second boy could come behind his brother and cover the hill where the corn had been planted. The first brother rises magically with the corn, proves vitally resilient, and begins selling his roasting ears to the angels. He drops his sibling a note:

"Passed through Heaven yesterday at twelve o'clock sellin' roastin' ears to angels."[10]

How the Florida Land Turtle Got Its Name

Equally engaging is Hurston's humorous story of how the Florida land turtle, the gopher, got its name. This tale also appeared in the state guide and embellished the tour through Hurston's native area of central Florida. A version of the tale can be found in *Mules and Men*, but her FWP tale adapts names and animals more specifically to the Florida setting.[11]

■ ■ ■

The tale opens with the picturesque scene of God sitting on Tampa Bay making sea-things and throwing them into the water. His nemesis, the Devil, happens by, looks at what God is doing, and brags that he can do the same. God told him that he couldn't, but told him to try anyway. But try as he may, the Devil was unsuccessful. His sea-thing, meant to be a turtle, refused to stay in the water. Upon seeing it God said, "This ain't no turtle what yo' done. But to show I'm fair-minded, I'll blow the breath of life into it for you." And with that, God blew life into the turtle. But the ill-made creature refused to stay in the water. "I told you [you] couldn't make no turtle," said God. "A turtle is a sea-thing an' lives in the water, an' this thing you made won't even stay no longer than he can swim out," God added. The Devil, realizing he couldn't out-argue God, quipped, "Well, if it ain't no turtle, it'll go fer one sure enough, and folks'll eat him for a turtle." From then on "go fer" came to be the animal's name. As was the case in many African American tales, the Devil had the last laugh. His humor, pitted against God's, triumphed again. This ironic play on words remained a common element in African American humor.

Uncle Monday

The land turtle was a familiar sight in Florida, but the alligator was an even more commanding presence. "Uncle Monday" enshrines the power and might of this Florida symbol, while at the same time combining the African influence of hoodoo.

This tale concerns Uncle Monday, the powerful African hoodoo doctor who could turn himself into an alligator. Only an eight-line excerpt from Hurston's several pages appeared in the guidebook, under the town history of Eatonville. Placed just after "Eatonville When You Look at It," the story fulfilled guide goals to illustrate local history and life. It focuses on Uncle Monday's fateful influence on the villagers. This tale was one the old folks told, one that Hurston had heard most of her life. Adapted to the guidebook context, the tale presents a "legendary alligator," "Eatonville's most celebrated resident," and what was claimed to be "the world's largest alligator."[12] This was just the sort of fare on which Florida tourists of the 1930s feasted.

This version extends the tales of Uncle Monday that appeared in Nancy Cunard's *Negro: An Anthology* (1934) and it was reprinted in Toni Cade Bambara's *The Sanctified Church*. The FWP tale enlarges Uncle Monday's early history, giving details about his slave background, participation in the Seminole Wars, and fateful residence in Lake Belle.

Hurston's FWP version, which has remained all these years in state files, unfolds on two levels. On the surface level, we have the elements of dramatic narration: strong characters, a good story line, and a vibrant ending. On a deeper level, the folktale was a powerful teaching tool, instructing present and future generations about the consequences of pride and arrogance.

■ ■ ■

Uncle Monday was the name he told the people, so that is all anybody knew to call him. The talk about him is mixed up with both Eatonville and Maitland. Eatonville for a number of reasons, and Maitland because that is where the lake is.

They say that when Uncle Monday is not a man, he is the big

alligator that lives in Lake Belle. That when he goes back to join the waters there is bellowing and turmoil among the gators all night long in the lake. The brutes are acknowledging his mastery and paying homage. He has ruled and been king since the days of the haughty Osceola. Uncle Monday was a great African medicine man that got captured and sold into slavery but soon made his escape from a rice plantation in Georgia or South Carolina and made his way down into the Indian country which is now Florida. He made medicine among them with the escaped slaves and fought as fiercely as the best against the white man's arms. But by reason of one disaster or another, the Indian–Negro forces were pushed south and south and south. The war party with which Uncle Monday was fighting made its last stand around Fort Maitland. For the dark-skins that day there was nothing but dying and fleeing. But not for Uncle Monday. He assembled all that was left of the forces on the shore of Lake Belle. They had been driven from the shore of Lake Maitland. What is now Lake Belle was deep in a forest. Uncle Monday announced to the remains of the army that in Africa he had belonged to the crocodile clan. He had been advised that all was lost, so far as their resistance to the white man's arms was concerned. He would go to join his brothers and wait. Someday he would come again and walk these shores in peace. So before them all he made a great ceremony, drummed and danced to the rhythm beat out by blacks, danced until his face grew longer and very terrible, till his arms and legs began to change, until his skin grew thicker and scaly and his voice came like thunder. And from the lake came alligator voices to answer his own. A thousand gators swept up to the banks of the lake and made a lane between the ranks and he glided majestically into the water between the rank and file of thundering gators and they disappeared after him. That was the way he left the land, and they tell many stories of how he came back.

Anyhow, when he lived in a tiny hovel on the shore of Blue Sink, Old Judy Bronson felt pangs of professional jealousy. She kept saying with more and more passion that the awe and worship showered on Uncle Monday was going to waste. She said that he was not even as good a hoodoo doctor as she was, and what was more, work that he might do, she could not only undo it, she could and would "throw it back on him." That statement insinuates a great deal of power indeed. Nobody ever heard Uncle Monday say one word about it one way or another, except to comment when he was told about it one night for the hundredth time, "The foolishness of tongues is higher than mountains." He made no move to "prove and fend" about Old Judy's slander at all.

But one late afternoon, Judy told her half-grown grandson to fix her a pole so that she could go fishing. This was startling to all of her family, for she had given up going fishing years ago and said repeatedly that she could not be bothered sitting on fishing ponds and having the red bugs and the mosquitoes eating her old carcass up. So they were surprised but not pleased when she ordered somebody to dig her some bait and rig up a pole for her to go fishing all by herself around sundown. Neither did they like the idea of her going to Blue Sink Lake, which is deep and bottomless only a few steps from shore almost everywhere around it. They tried to stop her, but she cut them off short with, "I just got to go, so hush up jawing and do like I told you." So the old woman went against herself down to Blue Sink to fish that sundown.

She said nothing but [baited] her hook and she soon wanted to go especially since before she could get her hook baited and get it into the water, it was nearly dark. She didn't like to walk through the brush anyway after it got too dark to see where she was going, but somehow she could not get the consent of her mind to get up and run like she wanted to. Look like she felt the dark slipping up on her and grabbing hold of her like a varmint.

When the dark was finally there for good, she got so scared that she lost use of herself about the legs. Then she heard a wind start up the hill a little way off and come rushing down upon her and the lake and in the twinkling of an eye she found herself falling into the lake. And she was so afraid!! She had always been afraid of water and darkness even when they were separate things. And the two together were more terrible than she could find words to tell afterwards. And both of these elements held her in their claws. She was in the lake, terrible Blue Sink, and she could not get out. She was afraid to struggle for fear that she would slip off into the deeps. Or some foul varmint might be attracted to her struggles and get her. But she could not stay there either, so she began to try to get to her feet and found out that she had no power at all in her limbs. It was all that she could do to support herself on her hands to keep her head above water. Finally she found the power to scream for help. Maybe somebody in the far-off village might hear her cry. But the moment that the squall left her lips, something huge hovered over her and the water and told her, "Hush! Your tongue, your bragging, lying tongue, has brought you here and here you will stay until I decide for you to leave." Judy could make out nothing of form and outline in the darkness, but she swore that it was the voice of Uncle Monday. Then a brilliant beam of light fell clear across the lake like a flaming sword, and she saw Uncle Monday walking across the lake from the opposite side to where she was and in the luminosity on either side of the reddish ray, the light ray that pointed dead at her from the opposite side of the lake like a monster spear made out of light, swam a horde of alligators like an army behind their leader. Uncle Monday was dressed in strange clothes and he walked proudly like a king down that shimmering band of light to where she laid there in the edge of the lake and about to drown and die of terror. "When you quit putting your ignorance and your weakness against me, you can get out of the water. I put you here and here you will stay until you bow down and acknowledge." Old Judy say she fought against it in her mind because she hated the man or whatever he was for stealing away her living and her prestige in the community. But fear rode her down. "I am going, but I shall leave a messenger and a guard. When you bow down somebody will find you, but not until." Then the light on the lake began to fade until it was gone and the man and his swimming escort was gone. There was a slight disturbance in the water and a huge alligator glided up beside her and stationed himself motionless along beside her so close that she could not help touching him when she breathed. Then her will gave away, and she was willing to bow down and acknowledge that she was weak and nothing beside Uncle Monday. She could not have done even a hundredth part of what she had seen and felt tonight. So inside she began to beg for mercy. Then she said it out loud, and almost at once she saw a flambeau moving down the hill towards the water and she heard her grandson calling her and telling the rest that she just had to be around there some place because he knew she had come to this lake. So she made a sound and they found her.

Her folks kept telling Judy that she had had a stroke and fallen in the lake and imagined all the rest of it. But to the day of her death she maintained that it all really happened. So she never fooled with hoodoo work anymore, and she never made any more slighting remarks about Uncle Monday again. She gave up the doctor's medicine and sent for him to put her on her feet again, and she did walk around a little while before she died.

Roy Makes a Car

Not all of Hurston's folk tales written for the Florida guidebook were published. Just as the extended version of "Uncle Monday" remained in the files, so too did her strikingly clever story "Roy Makes a Car." The contemporary nature of the story suggests that Hurston overheard local people talking and joking about Roy Tyle and his ability to tinker and invent. Stetson Kennedy, her contemporary on the FWP, seemed to think she drew stories directly from the people and wrote them out.[13]

Perhaps the tale was not included because it was more creative than traditional. With guidebook space at a premium, descriptions of local events and geographical places preempted imaginative pieces like "Roy Makes a Car." The tale demonstrates the continual impulse of the people to adapt modern-day happenings to the folkloric experience.

■ ■ ■

Roy Tyle runs the Maitland garage in Orange County. He is a celebrated mechanic, and many tales are told about his prowess with tools. He is a local Vulcan with his forge. They talk about him like this:

Roy, you know, made an automobile one time because he couldn't find one nowhere made to suit him. He said that if a car was made right there wouldn't be none of these collisions on curves. So the people wanted to know how he was going to stop it. He said if they give him time, he would show them that collisions wasn't nothing but foolishness. So he went back inside his garage with his working tools and wrenches and went to work. So after a while he told them he was ready to show his low-compression-non-collision-riding-springs. So they brought out first one car and then another and met him on the curve and his car would just squat down when he pressed a button and just run right under them other cars. You just couldn't hit him. They tried big old Mack trucks and he just run right under them too. Then somebody went and got a Buick because it is so underslung and low to the ground that it looks like it's squatting down all the time because this man said he bet Roy's car couldn't squat under no Buick, but it sure did. So Roy took his car up north and sold it off for a whole lot of money and come on back home.

Well, way after while Roy got tired of just sitting around the place so he told his wife that he believed he wanted him another car. Too lonesome without something to ride in. So this time he took and made a car that had wings folded on top of it so he could just lift it around the curves so nothing couldn't hit him. Well, from flying his car around them curves he took to flying it right smart and finally he didn't drive it on the ground hardly at all. And that is just how he got rid of the thing, too. One day, you see, Roy was way up there in his car flying around and God seen that automobile and bought it off of Roy, and them angels ain't flew a lick since they got the model. They all riding around heaven in them new models been made from Roy's car. So Roy is back again working on something else. Lord knows what it will be next time. 'Tain't never no telling what Roy will make.

Florida Images

"Florida is a place that draws people," Hurston wrote in *Mules and Men.*[14] She, too, was continually drawn back to her "native" village for physical and psychological refreshment. All of her books were either written in or about Florida. As a federal writer, Hurston was again called upon to describe her native state. She, like other fieldworkers, followed guidebook instructions to "look with fresh eyes" at familiar places and people that she had "known most of her life."[15] For the guidebook Hurston wrote the town histories of Eatonville, Goldsborough, and Ocoee.[16] For the "Lexicon of Trade Jargon," she profiled the turpentine and citrus industries, giving an insider's view of these Florida trades.[17]

The Florida guidebook drew other Florida images from Hurston. A credited excerpt, taken from *Their Eyes Were Watching God* (1937), described town life in Pahokee, an agricultural trading center and shipping point for Florida's winter vegetable trade. It was here in the Lake Okeechobee area that migrants arrived during the January-to-April winter vegetable season to harvest the crops. What is remarkable about the inclusion of the Hurston passage is the raw, sordid portrait of the state that it conveys:

> Permanent transients with no attachments and tired-looking men with their families and dogs in flivvers. All night, all day, hurrying in to pick beans. Skillets, beds, patched-up spare inner tubes all hanging and dangling from the ancient cars on the outside, and hopeful humanity, herded and hovering on the inside, chugging on to the muck. People ugly from ignorance and broken from being poor.[18]

This life was economic and cultural worlds away from the ordinary Florida tourist's comfortable existence. Her commentary stands as one of the few guide passages that referred to the presence and condition of the state's migrant workers. Again, Washington's influence and Hurston's presence in the national office during the final editing of the book must be considered. Later events would show that state editors would not have afforded Hurston the honor of a credited excerpt.[19]

Two Towns

Every FWP field writer was asked to observe and write about daily life in the towns in the surrounding area. Zora Neale Hurston commented on two. The first piece, on Eatonville, was published in the guidebook as a part of "Tour 2," which took the traveler south along US 17 from Jacksonville through the Winter Park–Orlando area. The second, describing the defunct township of Goldsborough, remained in the files, and is published here for the first time.

■ ■ ■ ■ ■ ■ ■ ■ ■ ■ ■ ■

Eatonville When You Look at It

In the mid-1930s, Eatonville was a tiny hamlet of 136 souls, a town so small that it did not even claim a paved road. Motorists traveling through barely knew the town was there. Certainly, from the vantage point of cultural and economic interest, this small hamlet filled with working-class blacks held little cultural or economic interest for the white tourists traveling through. So why did the Florida guidebook devote so much space to Eatonville? The answer is found in Hurston's lyrical writing and her ability to give travelers a glimpse of the town's inner life. Hurston's impressions of her hometown provide an insider's view of what it was like to live in a tiny hamlet in the late 1920s and 1930s. Most of the landmarks that she describes no longer exist, so her description remains important as a historical record.

Displaying some of the best writing that went into the American Guide Series, "Eatonville When You Look at It" imparted to the reader the feeling of being there. Other fieldworkers' copy often was so heavily edited in the state office that it could no longer be identified as one writer's work, but Hurston's town history of Eatonville was published in the Florida guidebook just as she wrote it.[20]

■ ■ ■

Maitland is Maitland until it gets to Hurst's corner, and then it is Eatonville. Right in front of Willie Sewell's yellow-painted house the hard road quits being the hard road for a generous mile and becomes the heart of Eatonville. Or from a stranger's point of view, you could say that the road just bursts through on its way from Highway #17 to #441 scattering Eatonville right and left.

On the right after you leave the Sewell place you don't meet a thing that people live in until you come to the Green Lantern on the main corner. That corner has always been the main corner because that is where Joe Clark, the founder and first mayor of Eatonville, built his store when he started the town nearly sixty years ago, so that people have gotten used to gathering there and talking. Only Joe Clark sold groceries and general merchandise, while Lee Glenn sells drinks of all kinds and whatever goes with transient rooms. St. Lawrence Methodist church and parsonage are on that same side of the road between Sewell's and "the shop" and perhaps claim the souls of the place, but the shop is the heart of it. After the shop you come to the Widow Dash's orange grove, her screened porch, "double hips," and her new husband. Way down the end of the road to the right is Claude Mann's filling station and beyond that the last home in Eatonville, the big barn on the lake that is lived in by Zora Hurston.

Take the left side of the road and except for Macedonia Baptist church people just live along that side and play croquet in Armetta Jones's backyard behind the huge camphor tree. After the people quit living along that side of the road, the Robert Hungerford Industrial School begins and runs along the road for some distance so far as the land goes. The inadequate buildings stop short in the cleared land on the fringe of Eatonville proper. And west of it all, village and school, everybody knows that the sun makes his nest in some lonesome lake in the woods back there and gets his night rest.

But all of Eatonville is not on the hard road that becomes Apopka Avenue as it passes through town. There are back streets on both sides of the road. The two back streets on the right side are full of little houses squatting under hovering oaks. These houses are old and were made out of the town's first dreams. There is loved Lake Sabelia with its small colony of very modern houses lived in by successful villagers like Kelly Baldwin and the Williams. Away in the woody rises beyond Sabelia is Eatonville's Dogtown that looks as if it belonged on the African veldt. Off the road on the left is the brown with white trim modern public school with its well-kept yards and playgrounds that Howard Miller always looks after though he can scarcely read and write. They call this part of town Mars Hills as against Bones Valley to the right of the hard road. They call the tree-shaded land that runs past the schoolhouse West Street and it goes past several minor groves until it passes Jim Steele's fine orange grove and dips itself into Lake Belle, which is the home of Eatonville's most celebrated resident, the world's largest alligator.

Goldsborough

Located not far from Eatonville, Goldsborough had been another all-black, self-governing, incorporated town. But unlike Eatonville, Goldsborough came to the end of its history in 1911 when much larger and more powerful Sanford, in need of Goldsborough's land for expansion, engineered the revocation of its charter and incorporated its land for its own use.

Hurston took on the assignment of writing about a town that had not existed for nearly three decades. Why did she do this, knowing full well the piece's chances of being published were slim? For her, Goldsborough stood as a symbol of Jim Crow realities. It showed whites exercising their power at the cost of black people's independence. While Hurston says the reason for the charter revocation was not that the town was "colored," she shows how racial issues can be used to achieve economic goals. By writing the piece, Hurston was identifying with the still-seething rancor of black residents (whom she had clearly interviewed). Recounting this tragic injustice was a way to ease the burden, set the record straight, and perhaps protect Eatonville from a similar fate.

"Goldsborough" was never published. Hurston's field copy remained in the files. Yet from a vantage point of over half a century, it testifies, as only Zora Neale Hurston could, to the tragedy and duplicity of the Jim Crow South.

■ ■ ■

This former town is now known as West Sanford and is a part of the city of Sanford. It was incorporated as the Negro town of Goldsborough in December 1891 and ended as a town in 1911.

William Clark had been running a store in the Negro settlement there in 1886, and it was through his efforts that the incorporation came about. He was not the first mayor, however. On the first Monday in December 1891, Walter Williams was elected mayor of the town, with John Wesley Small, clerk of the court, William Clark, policeman.

The next year the town opened a school, with Katie Stubbins as the first teacher.

The site of the town was one-half mile square from Clark Street on the east to Mulberry on the west to Tenth Street on the north to Harrison Street on the south.

John Wesley Small was the first postmaster, and William Clark built the first house. Zion Methodist was the first church.

The thriving city of Sanford looked with displeasure on the new town, not because it was colored, but because it was incorporated, and thus would seem to block the westward expansion of Sanford. Many efforts were made to induce the Negro town to give up its charter, but to no avail. It became a source of great irritation to the bigger Sanford enthusiasts, but it seemed that nothing could be done about it. It remained for Forest Lake, then state senator from Orange County, to find a solution. He induced the legislature to rule that since that body had the right to grant a charter, they also had the right to take one back. They voted to take back the charters of both Sanford and Goldsborough. Then Sanford speedily reorganized itself and included the

Goldsborough tract in their next application for a charter, which was speedily granted. Thus ended the existence of the second incorporated Negro town in Florida. The city of Sanford promised to pay $10,375.90 to cover the indebtedness of Goldsborough. That is, they assumed the debts of the town, but nothing has come of it so far. William Clark is an old man who cherishes a mass of jumbled yellow papers all about the debt that he and some others hope to collect someday. But busy Sanford selling millions of dollars' worth of celery every season has forgotten all about those papers years ago.

Turpentine

Sometime in late spring 1939, Hurton was sent to Cross City, Florida, on a number of assignments. This wild, lawless town was situated on Florida's west coast, in the state's lumber-and-turpentine-producing region. It proved a fertile field for folklore research. In addition to scouting informants for the soon-to-arrive WPA Joint Committee on Folk Art recorders, Hurston was to obtain life histories of turpentiners for the newly inaugurated life history program.[21] The idea behind the life histories was to let the people speak in their own words to the rest of the nation and sharpen understanding of Southern life.

As one of the best writers and ablest field researchers, Hurston was expected to find telling subjects to interview among the black turpentiners. Through her past field experience, she had developed a quick eye for finding a good story. She knew how to become one of the people, gain their confidence, and get them to talk.

"Turpentine," intended as a life history, describes a ride through the woods with John McFarlin, a turpentine woods rider in the employ of the Aycock and Lindsay Company of Cross City. In it, Hurston departs from the life history format and frames the piece from her own point of view. Her reasons are her own, but more than likely she had seen a good story, and like any good writer shaped it her own way. Nearly a decade later, she drew from this experience in writing her novel *Seraph on the Suwanee*.

■ ■ ■

Well, I put on my shoes and I started. Going up some roads and down some others to see what Negroes do for a living. Going down one road I smelt hot rosin and looked and saw a "gum patch." That's a turpentine still to the outsider, but gum patch to those who work them.

It was not long before I was up in the foreman's face talking and asking to be talked to. He was a sort of pencil-shaped brown-stained man in his forties and his name was John McFarlin. He got to telling and I got to listening until the first thing I knew I was spending the night at his house so I could "ride the wood" with him next morning and see for myself instead of asking him so many questions. So that left me free to ask about songs of the turpentine woods.

"No, ma'am, they don't make up many songs. The boys used to be pretty bad about making up songs but they don't do that now."

"If you don't make up songs while you are working, don't you all make some up round the jook?"

"No, ma'am, it's like I told. 'Tain't like sawmills and such like that. Turpentine woods is kind of lonesome."

Foreman McFarlin had me up before five o'clock next morning. He had to wake up his camp and he always started out at five-thirty so that he had every man on the job by six.

Every man took his tools, went to his task—whatever he was doing when he knocked off at five-thirty that afternoon before, he got right on it in the morning. The foreman had eighteen men under him and he saw everyone in his place. He had five chippers, seven pullers, and five dippers, and a woodchopper. All the men off to work, John McFarlin straddled his horse, got one for me, and we began riding the wood. Talking about knowing his business! The foreman can ride a "drift" and with a glance tell if every "face" on every tree has been chipped.

First he rode a drift of virgin boxes. That is when a tree is first worked; it is a virgin box for three years. That is the finest rosin. The five men were chipping away. The chipper is the man who makes those little slanting cuts on pine trees so the gum exudes, and drains down into the box. He had a very sharp cutting tool that was heavily weighted in the handle and cunningly balanced so that he chips at a stroke. The company pays a cent a tree. We stopped and watched Lester Keller chip because he is hard to beat anywhere in the world. He often chips seven hundred or more trees a week.

A puller is a specialized chipper. He chips the trees when they have been worked too high for the chipper. He does this with a chipping ax with a long handle known as a puller. The foreman explained that the trees are chipped three years and pulled three years, then abandoned. Leroy Heath is the champ puller.

He inspected a drift that was being dipped. The men who dip take the cup off the tree, scrape out the gum with the dipping iron, and put it back in place and pass on to the next face. The dippers are paid eighty-five cents a barrel for gum, and ten barrels a week is good dipping. Dan Walker is the champ. He can dip two barrels a day.

The woodchopper cuts wood for the still. Wood is used to fire the furnace instead of coal because the company owns millions of cords of wood for burning in trees that have been worked out.

McFarlin explained that there is no chipping and dipping from November to March. In November they stop working the trees, scrape the faces, hoe and rake around the trees as a caution against fire.

The foreman gets $12.50 a week, the foreman's house, all the firewood he wants, and all the gardening space he wants.

The Citrus Industry

Shortly after joining the FWP, Hurston was sent out into the field to obtain detailed information about the citrus industry. She did not have to travel far. Eatonville was surrounded by orange groves, and many of the area's residents worked in them, including John C. Hamilton, known by the nickname "Seaboard." In order to obtain firsthand knowledge of the industry, Hurston interviewed Seaboard, reputed to be the fastest orange picker in the county, and she submitted her report.[22] Seaboard was an old acquaintance. He had been one of her folkloric sources for *Mules and Men* and at the time of the interview was courting her niece Wilhelmina, whom he later married.

Hurston's exchange with Seaboard conveys much more detail and positive feelings about the trade than did other interviews conducted with grove workers as a part of the life history program. Others felt exploited. Horace Thomas, another grove worker, confided to one federal writer, "You know, ma'am, we is victims of those what has got the money."[23]

It is quite possible that part of Hurston's interview with John C. Hamilton could have been intended for the proposed "Lexicon of Trade Jargon," which was to detail language used in unusual trades. Although that publication never materialized, much of the information found in Hurston's interview with Seaboard found its way into the tour section of the Florida guidebook detailing that area of the state.

■ ■ ■

John C. Hamilton is a streamlined young colored man, known among his associates by the nickname of "Seaboard" and reputed to be the fastest orange picker in Florida.

John says:

Of the Florida oranges, the first to mature is the Hemline, which ripens in September; the second is the Parson Brown; the third, the Pineapple; the fourth, the Scaly, which grows on very tall trees; and the last is the Valencia, ripening the latter part of May. The work of picking starts in mid-September and lasts to the end of the following June.

There are two main varieties of grapefruit, the Marsh seedless, a small fruit, and the Common, an early variety. Then there are other citrus, the tangerines, satsuma, tangelos, tango range, etc. We do not really pick oranges. They are cut with a pair of clippers. These are like shears or medium-sized scissors, with the points curved and bent down. The man mounts the ladder, takes hold of a twig with his left hand, and cuts the fruit from the twig with the clippers, and it falls into a bag which has a stiff hook to keep it open, the bag being strapped to the cutter's shoulders. When the bags are filled, they are dumped into field boxes of two bushels' capacity and picked up by a truck dubbed a "rowley" because it works in the field; the other truck which carries the workers back and forth is called the "road truck."

There are two loaders to a crew of cutters, and they receive thirty-five cents per hour for loading the boxes on the "rowley." The cutters receive six cents per box for their work, except when picking from seedlings, which are very tall trees, when they get nine cents per box. The long ladders used to reach the top of the seedling trees are called "dead reds," because they are so heavy.

The small trees in the nursery are called "cutting buds." Now most of the groves are budded, as these mature in three years and start bearing. The buds are grafted to the hardy sour orange stock. They require careful cultivation and are easily hurt by the cold. The seedlings are much hardier, withstand considerable frost, and are preferred by grove owners on account of the lesser risk, but take seven years to reach the bearing stage. A seedling grove is more valuable and sells for a much higher price than a budded grove.

There are many blacksnakes in citrus trees and often rattlesnakes on the ground, since they like open spaces, but the bane of the orange pickers is the grampus, a kind of scorpion, with a stinger in its tail, often found in rotten wood in the groves.

The grove owner attends to the planting, cultivation, pruning, spraying, and fertilizing of a grove. Then when the season opens, experienced buyers come out from the packing houses and bid on the possible output of the grove. If the buyer estimates five hundred boxes, he makes a price on that quantity, usually around $1.75 per box. However, if the grove produces in the season six hundred or seven hundred boxes, that is the owner's loss.

The cutters are hired by the packing house, and are transported together with the loaders, from grove to grove, sometimes being carried a distance of seventy-five miles to their work.

There are also cooperative groups. There is one which operates the "Avalon Grove" near Howey-in-the-Hills, in which around two hundred people are stockholders. The Florida Fruit Exchange, a company of growers, will plant a small grove from five acres up, taking the first crop to settle the debt, and after that, spray, prune, and market the crop, taking a share for their work.

The Packing House

Women do all the packing. The fruit is sorted and graded into sizes by machinery, also sprayed mechanically with the vegetable coloring matter. All the women have to do is wrap the fruit and place it in the boxes. They are paid six cents for a box for oranges, four cents for a box for grapefruit, and eight cents per box for tangerines and the smaller fruit. The fast workers can make from five to six dollars per day. They have no regular starting time or quitting time, as all cars must be loaded, and the floors cleared of fruit each night before the day is closed. Sometimes they work until midnight and are on the job the next morning at eight. It is the same with the loaders in the groves. Each day's harvest must be taken care of before the loader can knock off, but by the end of the week, he often gets a paycheck running from thirty-five to forty-five dollars, but if one box is lost before it reaches the packing house, he has to pay for it.

No scales are needed, as there is no need at any time of weighing either the fruit or the boxes.

In all my experience in the groves, I have never seen a medfly. During the scare several years ago, when this pest was reported to have been found in Florida groves, I looked early and late, but never found one, although I saw crops ruined and groves destroyed. One man was supposed to have captured a medfly and put it in a bottle in his store, but it was only an ordinary housefly.

Squirrels, rats, and birds are sometimes troublesome in the citrus groves, as they especially like oranges and cut holes in them.

Freezes

In case of freezes the buyer has to protect the grove on which he has bargained for fruit, then the crew brings out the firepots, which are placed between the rows of trees. Fire is made, mostly of wood, though some use oil. The owner has nothing to do with it, as the buyer or packing house assumes all responsibility. I have seen frozen fruit sell in the groves at twenty-five cents per box.

In setting out the groves, however, windbreaks are planted on the north side, as well as the eastern sides, usually of Australian pines, as they grow rapidly, much faster than the citrus trees, and provide fine protection from cold.

As grove coverage, crotalaria is also planted, together with cowpeas and other similar crops, beggarweeds, the seeds for which are gathered and whole groves planted with it. A lake nearby or a body of water is thought also to provide protection from cold, on account of the evaporation of the water. Some of the better-kept groves are equipped with irrigation facilities, with pipes laid along the ground from artesian wells, often the pieces being even joined together. This irrigation is a great advantage, as in dry seasons like the one just passed, the trees get so parched for water that when the rains start again, they begin to bloom, and a June bloom, like that of this year, retards the production.

The Day's Work

When a cutter starts working for the packing house, he is given a number according to his registration on the payroll. My number this year is 42, and I carried it throughout the season. We go to the grove around seven-thirty A.M., and each man's number is placed in a hat. The foreman draws out the numbers, and if my number comes first, I have to take the first row of trees, and so on down the line. The first rows, the trees on the north side, do not bear as well as those in the middle of the grove, so all cutters like to draw the middle rows, where fruit is plentiful and bags fill up quickly. As I fill up a box I place number 42 on a ticket and put it in the box. The foreman gathers up the tickets, and at the end of the day, I get credit for the proper number of boxes. The day ends around six to six-thirty P.M. When a cutter finishes his own row, he helps others who have not completed their rows.

The workers sing in the groves, mostly blues songs about women and likker. The man from the packing house is called the superintendent. All he does is to go out and buy up groves. The foreman is called the field foreman. He counts the number of boxes. Sometimes we get mad at him, but we are careful not to *call* him anything.

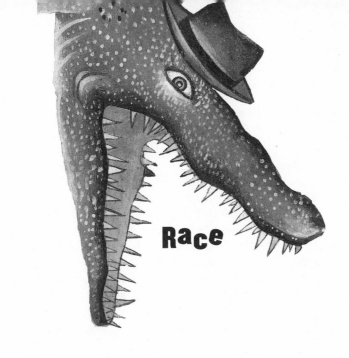

Race

The first selection in this section, "Art and Such," intended for the art and literature chapter of *The Florida Negro*, frames Hurston's ideas as to why blacks had not by the late 1930s made more progress in the arts. She bemoans the fact that attention on race and its "suffering" choked back "the song of morning." The essay focuses on the hazards of such a stance. The essay goes on to profile the artistic accomplishments of prominent black Floridians, and Hurston devotes considerable space to the promotion of her own literary point of view.

The second selection, "The Ocoee Riot," documents the heinous affair that took place in Ocoee in 1920. In a reportorial tone, Hurston tells the entire story from the point of view of the town's black population. It is interesting to compare this event with an equally tragic one that similarly ended in black residents' deaths, the now infamous Rosewood Massacre, which took place on the west coast of central Florida. Unlike Rosewood residents, the townspeople of Ocoee returned to their homes. Both incidents were part of the hideous realities of the Jim Crow South.

Art and Such

During the fall of 1938, Hurston was assigned the writing of the art and literature chapter for *The Florida Negro*. Her task could have been a simple one—a mere summary of notable black Floridians' literary and artistic achievements. However, Hurston departed from her assignment's rather narrow focus and began with an indictment of the attitudes that, she believed, had retarded African American's progress in the arts.

In "Art and Such," Hurston puts forth her belief that black life in all its manifestations, not merely race relations, should be the subject of black literature. In essence, she claims the freedom for black writing that white writing enjoyed—the independence to write about the interior life and relations within a community.

Only in the last pages of the essay does Hurston attempt to fulfill her assignment's purpose, and she devotes more space to herself than to any of the other black artists she mentions. Her critique of her own writing, which she believes furthered African Americans' position in the arts, is of special interest. Although the essay did not serve Federal Writers' Project purposes, it remains a stout defense of Hurston's own literary stance.

■ ■ ■

When the scope of American art is viewed as a whole, the contribution of the Negro is found to be small, that is, if we exclude the anonymous folk creations of music, tales, and dances. One immediately takes into consideration that only three generations separate the Negro from the muteness of slavery, and recognizes that creation is in its stumbling infancy.

Taking things as time goes we have first the long mute period of slavery during which many undreamed-of geniuses must have lived and died. Folk tales and music tell us this much. Then the hurly-burly of the Reconstruction and what followed when the black mouth became vocal. But nothing creative came out of this period because this new man, this first talking black man, was necessarily concerned with its newness. The old world he used to know had been turned upside down and so made new for him, [and it] naturally engaged his wonder and attention. Therefore, and in consequence, he had to spend some time, a generation or two, talking out his thoughts and feelings he had during centuries of silence.

He rejoiced with the realization of old dreams and he cried new cries for wounds that had become scars. It was the age of cries. If it seems monotonous one remembers the ex-slave had the pitying ear of the world. He had the encouragement of Northern sympathizers.

In spite of the fact that no creative artist who means anything to the arts of Florida, the United States, nor the world came out of this period, those first twenty-five years are of tremendous importance no matter which way you look at it. What went on inside the Negro was of more importance than the turbulent doings going on external of him. This postwar generation time was a matrix from which certain ideas came that have seriously affected art creation as well as every other form of Negro expression, including the economic.

Out of this period of sound and emotion came the Race Man and Race Woman; that great horde of individuals known as "Race Champions." The great Frederick Douglass was the original pattern, no doubt, for these people who went up and down the land making speeches so fixed in type as to become a folk pattern. But Douglass had the combination of a great cause and the propitious moment as a setting for his talents and he became a famous man. These others had the wish to be heard and a set of phrases as they became Race Men or Women as the case might be. It was the era of tongue and lung. The "leaders" loved to speak and the new-freed field hands loved gatherings and brave words, so the tribe increased.

It was so easy to become a Race Leader in those days. So few Negroes knew how to read and write that any black man who was proficient in these arts was something to be wondered at. What had been looked upon as something that only the brains of the master-kind could cope with was done by a black person! Astonishing! He must be exceptional to do all that! He was a leader, and went north to his life work of talking the race problem. He could and did teach school like white folks. If he was not "called to preach" he most certainly was made a teacher and either of these positions made him a local leader. The idea grew and traveled. When the first Negroes entered Northern colleges even the Northern whites were tremendously impressed. It was apparent that while setting the slaves free they had declared the equality of men, they did not actually believe any such thing except as voting power. To see a Negro enter Yale to attempt to master the same courses as the whites was something to marvel over. To see one actually take a degree at Harvard, let us say, was a miracle. The phenomenon was made over and pampered. He was told so often that his mentality stood him alone among his kind and that it was a tragic accident that made him a Negro that he came to believe it himself and struck the tragic pose. Naturally he became a leader. Any Negro who graduated from a white school automatically became a national leader and as such could give opinions on anything at all in which the word Negro occurred. But it had to be sad. Any Negro who had all that brains to be taking a degree at a white college was bound to know every thought and feeling of every other Negro in America, however remote from him, and he was bound to feel sad. It was assumed that no Negro brain could ever grasp the curriculum of a white college, so the black man who did had come by some white folks' brain by accident and there was bound to be conflict between his dark body and his white mind. Hence the stultifying doctrine that has not altogether been laughed out of existence at the present. In spite of the thousands and thousands of Negro graduates of good colleges, in spite of hundreds of graduates of New England and Western colleges, there are gray-haired graduates of New England colleges still clutching at the vapors of uniqueness. Despite the fact that Negroes have distinguished themselves in every major field of activity in the nation some of the leftovers still grab at the mantle of Race Leader. Just let them hear that white people have curiosity about some activity among Negroes, and these "leaders" will not let their shirttails touch them (i.e., sit down) until they have rushed forward and offered themselves as an authority on the subject whether they have ever heard of it before or not. In the very face of a situation as different from the 1880s as chalk is from cheese, they stand around and mouth the same trite phrases, and try their practiced best to look sad. They call spirituals "Our Sorrow Songs" and other such tomfoolery in an effort to get into the spotlight if possible without having ever done anything to improve education, industry, invention, art and never having uttered a quotable line. Though he is being jostled about these days and paid scant attention, the Race Man is still with us—he and his Reconstruction pulings. His job today is to rush around seeking for something he can "resent."

How has this Race attitude affected the arts in Florida? In Florida as elsewhere in America this background has worked the mind of the creator. Can the black poet sing a song to the morning? Up springs the song to his lips but it is fought back. He says to himself, "Ah, this is a beautiful song inside me. I feel the morning star in my throat. I will sing of the star and the morning." Then his background thrusts itself between his lips and the star and he mutters, "Ought I not to be singing of our sorrows? That is what is expected of me and I shall be considered forgetful of our past and present. If I do not some will even call me a coward. The one subject for a Negro is the Race and its sufferings and so the song of the morning must be choked back. I will write of a lynching instead." So the same old theme, the same old phrases, get done again to the detriment of art. To him no Negro exists as an individual— he exists only as another tragic unit of the Race. This in spite of the obvious fact that Negroes love and hate and fight and play and strive and travel and have a thousand and one interests in life like other humans. When his baby cuts a new tooth he brags as shamelessly as anyone else without once weeping over the prospect of some Klansman knocking it out when and if the child ever gets grown. The Negro artist knows all this but he conceives that a Negro can do nothing but weave something in his particular art form about the Race problem. The writer thinks that he has been brave in following in the groove of the Race Champions, when the truth is, it is the line of least resistance and least originality—certain to be approved of by the "champions" who want to hear the same thing over and over again even though they already know it by heart, and certain to be unread by everybody else. It is the same thing as waving the American flag in a poorly constructed play. Anyway, the effect of the whole period has been to fix activities in a mold that precluded originality and denied creation in the arts.

Results:

In painting one artist, O. Richard Reid of Fernandina, who at one time created a stir in New York art circles with his portraits of Fannie Hurst, John Barrymore, and H. L. Mencken. Of his recent works we hear nothing.

In sculpture, Augusta Savage of Green Cove Springs is making greater and greater contributions to what is significant in American art. Her subjects are Negroid for the most part but any sort of preachment is absent from her art. She seems striving to reach out to the rimbones of nothing and in so doing she touches a responsive chord in the universe and grows in stature.

The world of music has been enriched by the talents of J. Rosamond Johnson, a Jacksonville Negro. His range has been from light and frivolous tunes of musical comedy designed to merely entertain to some beautiful arrangements of spirituals which have been sung all over the world in concert halls. His truly great composition is the air which accompanies the words of the so-called "Negro National Anthem." The bittersweet poem is by his brother James Weldon Johnson.

Though it is not widely known, there is a house in Fernandina, Florida, whose interior is beautifully decorated in original wood carving. It is the work of the late Brooks Thompson, who was born a slave. Without ever having known anything about African art, he has achieved something very close to African concepts on the walls, doors, and ceilings of three rooms. His doors are things of wondrous beauty. The greater part of the work was done after he was in his seventies. "The feeling just came and I did it" is his explanation of how the carpenter turned wood-carver in his old age.

In literature Florida has two names: James Weldon Johnson, of many talents, and Zora Neale Hurston. As a poet Johnson wrote scattered bits of verse, and he wrote lyrics for the music of his brother

Rosamond. Then he wrote the campaign song for Theodore Roosevelt's campaign, "You're Alright Teddy," which swept the nation. After Theodore Roosevelt was safe in the White House he appointed the poet as consul to Venezuela. The time came when Johnson published volumes of verse and collected a volume of Negro sermons which he published under the title of *God's Trombones*. Among his most noted prose works are *The Autobiography of an Ex–Colored Man*, *Black Manhattan*, and his story of his own life, *Along This Way*.

Zora Neale Hurston won critical acclaim for two new things in Negro fiction. The first was an objective point of view. The subjective view was so universal that it had come to be taken for granted. When her first book, *Jonah's Gourd Vine*, a novel, appeared in 1934, the critics announced across the nation: "Here at last is a Negro story without bias. The characters live and move. The story is about Negroes but it could be anybody. It is the first time that a Negro story has been offered without special pleading. The characters in the story are seen in relation to themselves and not in relation to the whites as has been the rule. To watch these people one would conclude that there were not white people in the world. The author is an artist that will go far."

The second element that attracted attention was the telling of the story in the idiom—not the dialect—of the Negro. The Negro's poetical flow of language, his thinking in images and figures, was called to the attention of the outside world. Zora Hurston is the author of three other books, *Mules and Men*, *Their Eyes Were Watching God* (published also in England; translated into the Italian by Ada Prospero and published in Rome), and *Tell My Horse*.

It is not to be concluded from these meager offerings in the arts that Negro talent is lacking. There has been a cruel waste of genius during the long generations of slavery. There has been a squandering of genius during the three generations since Surrender on Race.

So the Negro begins feeling with his fingers to find himself in the plastic arts. He is well established in music, but still a long way to go to overtake his possibilities. In literature the first writings have been little more than putting into writing the sayings of the Race Men and Women and champions of "Race Consciousness." So that what was produced was a self-conscious document lacking in drama, analysis, characterization, and the universal oneness necessary to literature. But the idea was not to produce literature—it was to "champion the Race." The Fourteenth and Fifteenth Amendments got some pretty hard wear, and that sentence "You have made the *greatest* progress in so and so many years" was all the art in the literature in the purpose and period.

But one finds on all hands the weakening of race consciousness, impatience with Race Champions, and a growing taste for literature as such. The wedge has entered the great mass and one may expect some noble things from the Florida Negro in art in the next decade.

The Ocoee Riot

The central Florida hamlet of Ocoee was a small citrus-producing town of roughly eight hundred souls, located not far from Eatonville. In the late 1930s, it resembled any other sleepy Southern hamlet, with its prosperous white section lined with old two-story frame houses and shaded by live oaks and its not too prosperous-looking black quarters. The town enjoyed a peaceful history until 1920, when during the Presidential election of that year it became the scene of such violent racial strife that in 1939, when the guide writers attempted to record the town's history, conflicting reports of the event still abounded. So volatile were residents' feelings that the state guidebook carefully included the two widely divergent accounts of the incident.

The first account, told from white residents' perspective, conflicts with Hurston's: "On election day, November 3, 1920, a race riot broke out at Ocoee, following a disturbance at the polls. One of several conflicting stories attributed the trouble to the fact that July Perry, Negro foreman of a large orange grove, appeared at the polls while intoxicated, brandishing a shotgun, and killed two officers sent to arrest him at his home." Hurston's account, from the black perspective, describes whites' perpetration of the violence and murders.[24]

Although Hurston was not living in the area at the time of the riot (she was a student at Howard University), she was able to construct a chronicle of unfolding events from the graphic testimony of eyewitnesses, many of whom lost family members as a result of the brutality. Drawing on these interviews, she described the unfolding incidents that led to the riots and the lynching of July Perry.

The Ocoee incident was not something that one would expect Zora Neale Hurston to chronicle, considering the vehement charges of contemporaries that she did not concern herself with racial injustice in her writings. And writing such incendiary material for the FWP was a bold act. Her account challenged white complacency about the brutal reality of lynching that plagued the Deep South. Liberals in Congress had been pushing during the 1930s for passage of an anti-lynching measure that would ensure federal enforcement, but without success. Hurston knew that in vividly documenting the atrocities at Ocoee and the needless suffering of helpless victims, she was informing the wider world of the violence perpetrated against blacks.

Only a few lines of the essay are found in the Florida guidebook, because of limited space. But the fact that *any* portion of her account appeared was extraordinary and indicative of support in the national office.[25] What follows is Hurston's full version.

■ ■ ■

This happened on election day, November 2, 1920. Though the catastrophe took place in Ocoee, and it is always spoken of as the Ocoee Riot, witnesses both white and Negro state that it was not the regular population of Ocoee which participated in the affair. It is said that the majority of whites of the community deplored it at the time and have refused to accept full responsibility for it since.

According to witnesses, the racial disorder began in Winter Garden, a citrus town about three miles from Ocoee. There had been very lively electioneering during the Harding campaign, and the Negroes who were traditional Republicans were turning out in mass at the polls. Some of the poor whites who are traditional Democrats resented this under the heading that the Negroes were voting jobs away from the local people. It was decided with a great deal of heat to prevent the blacks from voting, which was done. Over in Ocoee, the blacks and the whites were turning out to the polls with great enthusiasm and no trouble was contemplated. In the afternoon, however, many of the whites of Winter Garden came on over to Ocoee celebrating election day. Seeing the Ocoee Negroes swarming to the polls, they began to urge the Ocoee whites to stop them, citing the evil happenings of the Reconstruction. Finally [the blacks] were ordered away, but some of them persisted.

The first act of physical violence occurred when Mose Norman came up to the polls to vote in defiance of the warning for Negroes to keep away. He was struck and driven off. But he did not let the matter drop so easily. He got into his automobile and drove to Orlando, the county seat, to see one Mr. Cheney, a well-known lawyer there, and told him what was happening. He advised Mose Norman that the men who were interfering with the voting were doing so illegally and that it was a very serious matter indeed. He instructed Mose to return to Ocoee and to take the names of all the Negroes who had been denied their constitutional right to vote, and some say he advised Norman to also take the names of the whites who were violating the polls. Mose Norman returned to Ocoee and parked his car on the main street of the town near the place of polling and got out. While he was away from the car, some of the disorderly whites from Winter Garden went to the car and searched it and found a shotgun under the seat. When he returned to the car, he was set upon and driven off. His speedy footwork was the only thing that saved him from serious injury. When this got around, the Negroes generally stayed away from the polling place and began to leave town for the day. Two or three more were hustled and beaten, however, during the afternoon. Then the white mobs began to parade up and down the streets and grew more disorderly and unmanageable. Towards sundown, it was suggested that they go over to Mose Norman's house and give him a good beating for his officiousness and for being a smart-aleck. But someone going around the lake had seen him visiting July Perry, a very prosperous Negro farmer and contractor, and they decided come nightfall they would go to the home of Perry and drag Mose out and chastise him.

In the meantime, the Black Dispatch (grapevine) had published all that was happening and most of the Negroes had left town or hidden out in the orange groves. July Perry armed himself and prepared to defend himself and his home. His friends all took to the woods and groves and left him to his courage. Even his sons hid out with the rest. His wife and daughter alone remained in the house with him. Perhaps they were afraid to leave the shelter of the house. Terrible rumors were about. Two of the three churches had been burned. The whole Negro settlement was being assaulted. It was cried that Langmaid, a Negro carpenter, had been beaten and castrated. But one thing was certain: Mose Norman, who had been the match to touch off the explosion, could not be found. He had thoroughly absented himself from the vicinity. When asked by some of the Negroes why he had had the gun under the seat of his car, he explained that he was doing some clearing out at Tildenville for Mr. Saddler, and always had his gun handy for a little hunting. At any rate, no Negro except July Perry had maintained his former address. So night dusted down on Ocoee, with the mobs seeking blood and ashes and July Perry standing his lone watch over his rights to life and property.

The night color gave courage to many men who had been diffident during the day hours. Fire was set to whole rows of Negro houses and the wretches who had thought to hide by crawling under these buildings were shot or shot at as they fled from the flames. In that way Maggie Genlack and her daughter were killed and their bodies left and partially burned by the flames that consumed their former home. The daughter was far advanced in pregnancy and so felt unequal to flight, since there was no conveyance that she could get. Her mother would not leave her alone as all the others vanished out of the quarters. They took counsel together and the old woman and her pregnant daughter crept under the house to escape the notice of the mob. Roosevelt Barton died of fire and gunshot wounds when the barn of July Perry was put to flames. He had thought that that would be a good hiding place, but when the fury of the crowd swept over the Perry place, the barn was fired and when Roosevelt tried to rush out he was driven back by a bullet to die in the fire. But this only happened after a pitched battle had been fought at Perry's house, with July Perry against the mob.

He loaded his high-powered rifle and waited, at the same time unwilling to believe that the white people with whom he had worked and associated so long would permit the irresponsibles from Winter Garden to harm him or his things. Nevertheless he waited ready to do that which becomes a man. He could not know that the mob was not seeking him at all, that they had come there because they thought that Mose Norman was hiding about the place. Perhaps if the mob had not been so sure that Mose was there that it was unnecessary to ask, all might have been different. They might have called out to him and he might have assured them by word of mouth or invited them in to see for themselves. They did not know that Norman had only spent a few minutes at the Perry home and then fled away to the groves. So they there outside began the assault upon the front of the house to gain entrance and Perry defended his door with all that he could command. He was effective. The mob was forced to retreat, and considered what was best to do. It was decided that while some kept up the harassment at the front, others would force an entrance through the back. Never had any of the mob suspected that Perry was alone in the house. They thought from the steady fire that several Negroes were at bay in there. It was Sam Salsbury who took a running start and kicked the back door open. Perry had not expected this, but he whirled at once and began to shoot at the gaping mouth of the door. His daughter, terrified at this new danger, tried to run out of the door and was shot in the shoulder by her father, who had not expected her to run into the line of fire. But the next bullet struck Sam Salsbury in the arm and the rear attackers retreated. But not before Elmer McDonald and a man named Overberry had lost their lives. The council decided that reinforcements were necessary to take the place, so the whole fighting force withdrew. Some phoned to Orlando to friends to come and help. Some phoned to Apopka and to other points. Some went in cars to bring help. So there was a lull in the fighting for two or three hours.

July Perry had not gone unhurt. A bullet or two had hit him. So in the lull his wife persuaded him to leave. He was weak from his hurts, so she lent her strength to get him away from the house and far down into the cane patch where they felt he would not be found. When the reinforced mob came back the doors were open and the searchers found only Perry's wounded daughter there. They did nothing to harm her but began an intensive hunt for Perry. It was around dawn when they found him weak and helpless in his hiding place, and he was removed to the jail in Orlando. It was after sunup when the mob stormed the jail and dragged him out and tied him to the back of a car and killed him and left his body swinging to a telephone post beside the highway.

That was the end of what happened in Ocoee on election day, 1920.

Performance Pieces

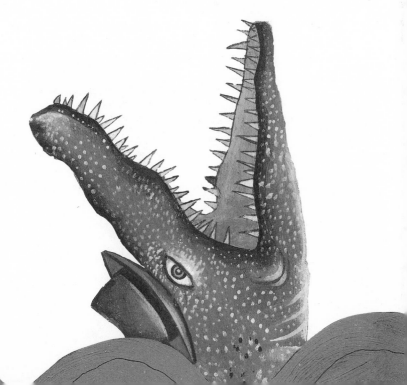

The WPA tapped Hurston's well-known dramatic talent to provide much-needed publicity and support for its relief programs. Prior to publishing her first book, Hurston sought drama as another vehicle by which she could bring genuine African American folklore to the public. She felt very passionately that the songs and dances of the people needed to be dramatized. Her American folkloric production *The Great Day*, performed January 10, 1932, at an off-Broadway theater, was the realization of that hope. Although it was a critical success, the show's inability to sustain itself financially (it must be remembered that January 1932 was the low point of the Great Depression) quickly brought down the curtain.[26]

In the coming months and years, Hurston re-created either all or parts of *The Great Day*, under various titles. The material contained in the selections in this section derived in one way or another from the field collecting presented in her off-Broadway production.

The first selection, "The Fire Dance," recreates the midnight scene from *The Great Day*. This short WPA performance includes three African dances—Jumping Dance, Ring Play, and Crow Dance—that announced the arrival of spring. In the program's playbill, Hurston noted that the dances were "brought to Florida by immigrant Negro workers from the Bahama Islands."

The second selection, "The Jacksonville Recordings," includes eighteen songs and the interview material that Hurston recorded for the WPA in June 1939. Of special note are her selection of songs and her comments about them. In the audio recording, she imitates the people's speech, such as the gamblers' talk as they sang "Let the Deal Go Down." Her voice conveys not only her enthusiasm but also her deep knowledge of the songs, the circumstances of their singing, and the people who sang them.

The Fire Dance

This Hurston-scripted performance, being published for the first time, was presented at the WPA's "National Exhibition of Skills" in Orlando from January 16 to February 16, 1939. The Federal Writers' Project titled it "The Fire Dance: An African Grotesque." These were the people's dances, and they show the survival of African traditions in African American culture. What is unusual is the federal government's versatility in sponsoring the arresting dances and presenting them as a part of its "new national folklore studies."[27]

■ ■ ■

There are thousands of Bahamians in south Florida, and nightly in the Everglades around the bean fields and sugar mills can be heard the pulsing of the dance drums. They are holding a "jumping dance." This is part of the dance cycle known as the Fire Dance. It is part of the celebration of New Year's from West Africa. They say that their ancestors told them that "on the Back" (Africa) when they see a certain tree put out new leaf, they know it is the New Year. So the *hougun*, or the priest, made a ceremonial fire and everyone went to the temple and got a torch of this sacred fire and went dancing to the crossroads. There every newcomer put his firebrand on the heap with the others and the dancing kept up all night. Maybe two or three days. It has three parts—the Jumping Dance; Ring Play; the Crow Dance.

Jumping Dance

The drum is heated over the fire and then turned, since the goat hide contracts when heated and tightens, thus giving a higher pitch. (The drum is beaten by hand.) There is a grand flourish of the drum—the circle forms, the drummer tears into a tune, and somebody starts to sing. The whole ring sings, claps hands, and some begin to "cut pork"—that is, make the introductory movements of the dance. Some bold person cuts pork and leaps out into the ring, does his or her "moves" (steps), chooses a partner, and retires. The rhythm is terrific! This dance is very much more difficult than it looks because the dancer must move on the drum. He or she must begin and finish each "move" according to the subtleties of the drum rhythm and tone, which is extremely varied. The dance has no point otherwise. Each dancer develops some particular "move" of his own. Naturally some are more talented than others and invent marvelous steps. These are recognized as the definite property of the inventor, and fights frequently break out at the theft of another's steps. The dance keeps up on the rhythm of the song being sung until the drum gets cold. When the drum is reheated, the tune changes.

There are one-jump tunes, two, and three.

A sample of the one-jump is:

Two banana, two!
Two banana, two!
Two banana, two!

On the first line, the dancer chosen "cuts pork." On the second, he is in the ring doing his move. On the third, he has chosen his partner (who is now cutting pork) and is on his way back to his place.

Full-Time Jump Song
(Cutting pork)
Bimi gal is a rock and a roller, never got a licking till you go down to Bimini
(Leaps into the ring)
Eh! Let me go down to Bimini!
Never get a licking till you go down to Bimini.

Ring Play

This is African rhythm with European borrowings. Group in ring as before. One dancer in center begins to sing and circle ring seeking a partner as the verse is being sung. At the very first beat of the refrain, the partner must join the seeker in the center and they do a duet rather than the solo dance of the "Jump." The hand-clapping is marvelous stop-time rhythm and the better the dancers the wilder the enthusiasm.

Song

(Solo dancer circling the inside of the ring seeking partner)
Mama I saw a sailboat
A-sailing in the harbor
I saw a yeller gal aboard it
And I took her to be my lover.
(Chosen one dances out in ring to meet other dancer)
Down the road, baby!
Two shillings in the cooker!
It's killing, mama!
It's killing mama!
Kiling mama! Killing mama!
(This keeps up until the dancers exhaust their repertoire of steps.
The one who was chosen stays in the ring and the other retires.
Begin all over the same routine.)
Peas and rice, throw it in the road,
Stand one side, make it three quarts,
Roll it, Roland, gimme some,
Roll it, Roland, gimme some! Etc.

Crow Dance

In the midst of the festivities, there is a change of drum tone and rhythm. The Crow Song begins and all look off to see the Crow make his entrance. It is a perfect rhythmic imitation of a buzzard flying and seeking food. He enters, finds food, takes some in his beak, and flies off. There is a bird in Africa worshiped similar to the hawk of the Egyptians.

Crow Song

SOLOIST: Oh! Ma-ma-ma come see dat crow!
CHORUS: See how he fly!
SOLOIST: Oh! Ma-ma-ma come see dat crow!
CHORUS: See how he fly!
SOLOIST: Dis crow, dis crow going to fly tonight!
CHORUS: See how he fly!
SOLOIST: Dis crow, dis crow going to fly tonight!
CHORUS: See how he fly!
SOLOIST: Oh! Ma-ma-ma come see dat crow, etc.
   (Until crow makes his screaming exit)

The dancers costume themselves to represent human beings, birds, animals, and even trees. In short, all nature is taking part in spring. All nature is choosing itself a partner. So the movements of the dance say something about the procreation of life.

The Jacksonville Recordings

Presented here is the transcription of Hurston's interview and song material from the WPA's Jacksonville recording session in June 1939. While other voice recordings of Hurston exist, this one, conducted by folklorist Herbert Halpert, is the most extensive. The interviews reveal a great deal about Hurston's folklore field collecting experience, a bit about her representation of herself to contemporaries (she claims to be thirty-five years old, when in fact she is forty-eight), and something of the background of the songs.

Hurston's particular selection of folk songs, which is in itself significant, showcases those she believed most representative of Florida black folks' life, work, and recreation. The first group are railroad lining tunes sung by workers as they double-tracked Henry Flagler's Florida East Coast Railway. The singing liner who led the songs was critical to the work process. Hurston points out, "If he did not sing, the men would not work." Barbara Berry Darsey, a Miami FWP field writer, interviewed Bradly Eberhart, one of these singing liners, who explained to her the process and role of singing as the men laid the monster nine-hundred-pound rails:

> Now de hans, dey all ready on de track wif de bars under de line, and dey line on de rhyme. . . . On de fust line de boys got de bars under de line, de rail, I means, but we calls hit de line. Den on de second line ob de song dey come down hard, sit down on the bars we calls hit, and on de words what rhyme dey jerk de bars up and dat straightens de track.

Hey, hey, sit down boys
I tole ol Bob to he face
I buy my whiskey at another place

When I sung "Hey, hey, sit down boys" de hans got ready to go down hard on de bars, den jerk up on de words "face" and "place" and dat straightened de line ob de track. . . . Dem boys, dey just cain't line track ifen a song ain't set fur 'em.

Centering on work and play, these forthright tunes tell us what life was like for Florida's African American laborers during the early decades of the twentieth century. Used to accompany and spur on labor, they express perfectly the communal nature of both work and music. In these songs, the men reveal their innermost concerns and feelings. They sing of girlfriends back home, "bulldozing" women, the bossman, and going broke.

Following the railroad lining tunes are a number of selections that Hurston collected from Polk County lumber camps and migrant crop pickers around the Everglades.

■ ■ ■

Goin' to See My Long-haired Babe

Hurston: My name is Zora Neale Hurston. I was born in Eatonville, Florida. I am thirty-five years old. This song I am going to sing is a railroad song that I found on a railroad down near Miami. And it was sung to me by Max Ford, an old railroad employee on a construction gang.
Halpert: How long ago was that?
Hurston: That was in 1930.
Halpert: How did you happen to be going around getting songs?
Hurston: I was collecting folk material for Columbia University, Department of Anthropology, Columbia University.
Halpert: What's the song called?
Hurston: "Goin' to See My Long-haired Babe." It's a railroad spiking song and the rhythm is suited to the spiking of the hammers.

Halpert: Maybe you'd try to emphasize the approximate rhythm of how they would hammer the spikes by hitting against the table.

Oh Lula! (Hammer) Oh Gal! (Hammer)
Want to see you so bad.
CHORUS:
Goin' to see my long-haired babe,
Goin' to see my long-haired babe
Oh lawd I'm goin' cross the water
See my long-haired babe. (Hammer)

What you reckon Mr. Treadwell said to Mr. Goff
Lawd I believe I'll go south pay them poor boys off.
CHORUS:
Goin' to see my long-haired babe,
Goin' to see my long-haired babe,
Oh lawd I'm goin' cross the water
See my long-haired babe. (Hammer)
CHORUS:
Oh Lula! Oh Gal!
Want to see you so bad.

Hurston: Let those hammers ring, boys!

Halpert: You seem to be hitting down twice for the hammer. What is that?

Hurston: The two men face each other with the hammers and they call themselves breasters. They stand breast to breast. And one hammer comes down and the other one comes down.

Halpert: Immediately afterwards?

Hurston: Yes, one comes down (Hammer. Pause. Hammer.)

Halpert: I see. And how long is that between the double strokes?

Hurston: The minute that one goes down, the other one is on the upstrike and comes right down behind.

Halpert: Who does the singing?

Hurston: The singing liner. It's the man who doesn't work at all, and he walks up and down and gives the rhythm for the people to wait.

Halpert: Oh. Is this for a whole crew of men?

Hurston: A whole crew of men singing at one time, and the railroad has to pay the singing liner or else the men won't work.

Halpert: If you hear that, you only hear the one man singing on the whole section of track.

Hurston: Not all the time, because different ones had different verses they want to put in themselves. So they jump in and after he starts the song. But the singing liner always starts it.

Halpert: Well now, look, the only thing is that you were given a long piece of singing without the rhythm of the . . . hammer section. I want to know approximately how often that comes.

Hurston: Well they often . . . do that.

Ah, Mobile

Hurston: This song, I got it at Talahand, Florida, which is the railroad center in the northern part of Florida.

Halpert: When was this?

Hurston: I got this in 1935. I don't remember the man's name who sung it to me, but I got it at Talahand. It's a railroad camp.

Halpert: What kind of song is it?

Hurston: This is not exactly a song. It's a chant for the men lining. A rail weighs nine hundred pounds, and the men have to take these lining bars and get it in shape to spike it down, and while they are doing that, why they have a chant and also some songs that they use the rhythm to work it into place and then the boys holler bring them a hammer gang and they start spiking it down.

Ah, Mobile, ha!
Ah, in Alabama, ha!
Ah, Fort Myers, ha!
Ah, in Florida, ha!
Ah, let's shake it, ha!
Ah, let's break it, ha!
Ah, let's shake it, ha!
Ah, just a hair, ha!

Hurston: Bring them a hammer gang.

Halpert: I would like you to do that again, but this time when that happens, what do they call the irons that they use for it?

Hurston: They call it a lining bar.

Halpert: The lining bar when they work it doesn't hear the clink of it?

Hurston: They just say, "Ha!" You don't hear the lining bar because it is under the rail and they shove the rail with it, but you can't hear it.

Halpert: Do they hit against it?

Hurston: No, it's under it, you see, it's just like under it . . . it's a crowbar.

Halpert: Because over in Mississippi, they show you by hitting. The way they did it was by several men taking a short stick.

Hurston: Well, I've seen them put it between their legs, this way, and put it back. And they get used to this plane under the rail and then they "Ha! Ha!" Like that.

Halpert: Now what do they do? Are they pulling it back?

Hurston: Pulling it back, because they are moving it backwards.

Halpert: In other words, they have it underneath, and they are using the leverage to go forward.

Hurston: That's right, yes, all the men—because it's awful straining. . . .

Halpert: And about how many men are on the bar?

Hurston: Oh, it's sometimes about seven or eight on it at one time.

Halpert: Well, first you try it and sing it over again.

Hurston: All right. (She repeats the song)

Shove It Over

Hurston: This song they call "Shove It Over," and it is a lining rhythm, pretty generally distributed all over Florida. It was sung to me by Charlie Jones on the railroad construction camp near Lakeland, Florida.

Halpert: About how long ago?

Hurston: I gathered that in '33, 1933.

When I get in Illinois
I'm going to spread the news about the Florida boys.
  CHORUS:
Shove it over!
Hey! Hey! Can't you line it?

Ah, shack-er-lack-er-lack-er-lack-er-lack-er-lack-er-lack! UMH.
Can't you move it?
Hey! Hey! Can't you try?

Eat him up whiskers, and he won't shave
Eat him up a body, and he won't bathe
   CHORUS:
Oh the rooster chew tobacoo
The hen dip her snuff
The biddy can't do it but he struts his stuff
   CHORUS:
Here comes a woman walking cross the field
Her mouth smoking like an automobile.
   CHORUS:
The cap'n got a pistol
He tried to play bad
But I'm goin ta take it if it make me mad.
   CHORUS:

Halpert: This is again for lining?

Hurston: This is a lining rhythm.

Halpert: Now where is the moving?

Hurston: When they say "Shakalaka, shakalaka," like they are getting ready to pull back, and when they say "AHH," they shove the rail over.

Halpert: In other words, it's a part of that, so this song gives quite a lot of rest in between.

Hurston: A lot of rest in between.

Halpert: And a harder shove?

Hurston: And a harder shove! At "UH!" they all go.

Halpert: It seems to have different effect [than] the other line, lining one you gave, that one about Mobile.

Hurston: Yes. Some are short, some are long, just according to the mood of the liner, and the men work whatever song he sung. They work that rhythm. Now when the men are lining, they put the rail down, and then of course the captain, he squats straddle of it and looks down and he could tell when it is lined up in, in, in exact line with the others. If they carry it too far, the captain, he'll say, "Shove it over." And if they carry it too far, he'll say, "Stand it back." And when they get it exactly in line he'll tell them, "Join it ahead," but they done corrupted that to

"Jonahead." And all of them say "Jonahead" for "Join it ahead." So this song is about lining. And the rhythm goes to a lining bar. They puts this long steel bar, crowbar, between the legs and uh, and pull back on it.

Halpert: How are they standing to the rail?

Hurston: Their back is to the rail.

Halpert: In other words, they have to force up on the bar.

Hurston: Pulling up on the bar, they don't have to look at the rail because that is the captain's job, to see when it is right.

Halpert: How do they get it under the rail?

Hurston: They just push the flange of this lining bar under the rail and then pull back on it.

Halpert: Do they have to look back at it or do they just feel it?

Hurston: Oh, they just feel it, sometimes they look back, you know, but most the time, they can feel it and they send it back.

Halpert: You are explaining that there are different rhythms before. Are there any particular kind that are faster or slower ones that we could use?

Hurston: No particular time, except just the feeling of the singing liner, whatever song he starts, if it is a fast rhythm, if it is slower, well, they wait, you know, a little slower, but they get just as much work done, it seems, somehow or other.

Mule on the Mount

Hurston: This song I am going to sing is a lining rhythm and I am going to call it "Mule on the Mount," though you can start with any verse you want and give it a name. It is one of the most widely distributed work songs in the United States and it has innumerable verses and whatnot, about everything under the sun. And it is a lining rhythm, though they sometimes sing it in the jook houses, and doing any kind of work at all, chopping wood, and in lumber camps, everywhere. There is nowhere where you can't find parts of this song.

Halpert: Is it just a song, or did you hear it all over?

Hurston: The tune is consistent, but the verses, you know how things is, every locality you find some new verses everywhere.

Halpert: I mean, does it have the same core? Does it have "Kneel on the mount"?

Hurston: Well, there is some place I haven't heard that same verse, "Kneel on the mount," but there is no place that I don't hear some of the same verses.

Halpert: Where did you learn this particular way?

Hurston: Well, I heard the first verses, I got at my native village of Eatonville, Florida, from George Thomas.

Halpert: And is that the only version you're going to sing?

Hurston: The tune is the same. I am going to sing verses from a whole lot of places.

Halpert: All right.

Cap'n got a mule
Mule on the mount
Call him Jerry Ha!
Cap'n got a mule
Mule on the mount
Call him Jerry
Goin' ride him down
Lawd, lawd, ride him down.

I got a woman, she shakes like jelly all over
I got a woman, she shakes like jelly all over
Her hips so broad, lawd, lawd, her hips so broad Ha!

My little woman, she had a baby this morning
My little woman, she had a baby this morning
He had blue eyes, lawd, lawd, he had blue eyes.

And I told her, must be the hellfire cap'n Ha!
And I told her, must be the hellfire cap'n Ha!
Lawd he had blue eyes.

Oh don't you hear them, a cuckoo bird keep a hollerin' Ha!
Don't you hear them, a cuckoo bird keep a hollerin' Ha!
It look like rain, lawd lawd, it look like rain.

I got a rainbow wrapped and tied around my shoulder
I got a rainbow wrapped and tied around my shoulder
It look like rain, lawd, lawd, it look like rain.

I got a woman, she's pretty but she's too bulldozing
I got a woman, she's pretty but she's too bulldozing
She won't live long, lawd, lawd, she won't live long.

Halpert: When you hear that song or the other songs, about how many verses would a man have?

Hurston: Yes, sometimes they sing thirty and forty verses.

Halpert: Run continuously?

Hurston: It is one of these things that has just grown by instrumental repetition until it is, perhaps, it is the longest song in America. (Laughter)

Let the Deal Go Down Boys

Hurston: . . . I am going to sing a gambling song that I collected at Bartow, Florida. The men are playing a game called Georgia Skin. That was the most favorite gambling game among the workers of the South. And they lose money on the drop of a card—the fall of a card. And there is a rhythm to the fall of the card. After they get set with the two principals and the other people . . . called pikers . . . anybody who wants a special card, he picks it out and they call that "sickin' one in the rough."

Halpert: I think a better way to explain it is how the cards are given out and how the people are.

Hurston: Well you see they take a deck of cards and they shuffle it real good and watch the man to be sure he don't steal nothing, that is, that he don't set a club. There are four cards of every kind in the deck and when a card like the card you have selected [appears], you lose. Sometimes if you don't watch the dealer, he will shuffle three cards just like his own down to the bottom of the deck, so everybody falls before he does, and then he wins all the money.

Halpert: So what does he do? Is the dealer holding a deck of cards?

Hurston: He puts it on the table. They don't allow him to hold it because they are afraid he will steal. So he puts it on the table and turns over a card.

Halpert: Turns over a card?

Hurston: Card by card.

Halpert: Yea.

Hurston: And then the card just like yours, when it falls you lose. And so they holler when he gets all set and when the principals got their cards and all the pikers got theirs. And then the man will say, "You want them to put the bets down." And he will say, "Put the money on the wood and make the bet go good, and then put it in sight and save a fight." So they all get the bets down and then he starts. They'll holler, "Let the deal go down, boys, let the deal go down." And some of them will start singing.

Let the deal go down boys
Let the deal go down.
   (And another card falls off the deck)
When your card get lucky
You oughta get a rolling game

Let the deal go down boys,
Let the deal go down.

Hurston: (Simulating the shouts of a Georgia Skin game) A card done fell. There you go, Shorty, put up some more money.

I goin' back to 'bama
Won't be worried with you.
Let the deal go down boys
Let the deal go down.

Hurston: (Again simulating a conversation among the Georgia Skin players) There you done fell, Charlie. See, I can't catch nothin'. I can't even catch nobody lookin' at me. Yea, take another card. Take this queen. Oh, no, I don't play those gals until way late at night. Give me another card. I don't want no queen. Put up some more money. Put up some more money . . . Shorty. Let the deal go down, boys, let the deal go down. I don't got no money. Lawd, I ain't got no chance. There you go, Blue Front. I tell you about bettin' a card and tell a lie about it. Put up some more money.

Let the deal go down boys,
Let the deal go down.
I ain't had no trouble, lawd
Until I stopped by, yeah!
Let the deal go down boys,
Let the deal go down.

Uncle Bud

Hurston: "Uncle Bud" is not a work song. It is sort of a social song
for amusement, and it is so widely distributed it is growing all the time
by incremental repetition. And it is known all over the South. No matter where you go you can find verses of "Uncle Bud." And it is a favorite
song, and the men get to working, and every kind of work, and they just
yell down on "Uncle Bud." And nobody particular leads it. Everybody
puts in his verse when he gets ready. And "Uncle Bud" goes and goes
and goes.

Halpert: Is it sung before respectable ladies?

Hurston: Never. It is one of those jook songs. And the woman that
they sing "Uncle Bud" in front of is a jook woman.

Halpert: I thought you heard it from a woman! (Laughter)

Hurston: Yeah! I heard it from a woman. (Laughter)

Uncle Bud is a man like this
If he can't get woman goin' to use his fists
Uncle Bud, Uncle Bud, Uncle Bud, Uncle Bud, Uncle Bud.

Oh I am goin' to town and goin' to hurry back
Uncle Bud's somethin' I sure do like,
Uncle Bud, Uncle Bud, Uncle Bud, Uncle Bud, Uncle Bud.

Oh little cat, big cat, little bitty kittens
Goin' to work their tails if it don't start fittin'
Uncle Bud, Uncle Bud, Uncle Bud, Uncle Bud, Uncle Bud.

Uncle Bud's growin' corn that sure need workin'
Uncle Bud's got gals that sure need jerkin'
Uncle Bud, Uncle Bud, Uncle Bud, Uncle Bud, Uncle Bud.

Uncle Bud's got gals that got no hairs
Uncle Bud's got cotton that's got no squares
Uncle Bud, Uncle Bud, Uncle Bud, Uncle Bud, Uncle Bud.

Oh it ain't no use in you raisin' sand
You got to take that turd off Grandpa's land
Uncle Bud, Uncle Bud, Uncle Bud, Uncle Bud, Uncle Bud.

Oh who in Hell, the God damn nations
Hid this turd on Pa's plantation
Uncle Bud, Uncle Bud, Uncle Bud, Uncle Bud, Uncle Bud.

Oh little cat, big cat, playin' in the sand
Little cat fought like a natural man
Uncle Bud, Uncle Bud, Uncle Bud, Uncle Bud, Uncle Bud.

Uncle Bud's a man, a man in full
His nuts hang down like a Jersey bull
Uncle Bud, Uncle Bud, Uncle Bud, Uncle Bud, Uncle Bud.

Uncle Bud's got girls that's long and tall
And they rock their men from wall to wall
Uncle Bud, Uncle Bud, Uncle Bud, Uncle Bud, Uncle Bud.

Uncle Bud's got girls that's long and tall
And they rock their hips like a cannon ball
Uncle Bud, Uncle Bud, Uncle Bud, Uncle Bud, Uncle Bud.

Hurston: I know I know some more words, but right now I don't recall them.

Halpert: I think that is a very valuable contribution to society I think we're recording.

The Beaufort Boat

Hurston: "The Beaufort Boat" is a song from the Geechee country in South Carolina, but I heard it down in Florida from a Geechee that moved down in Florida. I forget her name right now.

Halpert: What kind of song is it?

Hurston: It is a dance song, and it has that Charleston rhythm. (Hurston renders the song in perfect dialect.)

Oh the Beaufort boat done come
Gotta put in the pot back yon
Gotta eat 'em up, gonna salt 'em down
Gotta eat 'em ala boom bye um
Et Et Et Et Et Et
Oh the Beaufort boat done come
Gotta put 'em in the pot back yon
Gotta chew em down
Gotta eat 'em ala boom bye um
Oh Et Et Et Et Et

Halpert: What kind of song is it?

Hurston: It is a dance song and they will clap their hands on it and sing.

Ever Been Down

Hurston: I going to sing the blues called "Ever Been Down," and I got it down at Palm Beach from a fellow name Johnny.

Halpert: When did you get it?

Hurston: I got it in 1933.

Halpert: Can you tell me how old a blues it is? How you happened to learn it?

Hurston: Well, it's one of those things that just go down all the jooks and that and it goes by incremental repetition, gaining a verse here and a verse there. And don't suppose anybody knows how old it is and when it started.

Ever been down
Been down so long
Oh weep like a willow
Mourn just like a dove
Weep like a willow
Mourn just like a dove

Go fly to the mountain
Light on the man I love
I'd rather be in Tampa
With a whippoorwill
Rather be in Tampa
With a whippoorwill
Than be round here hidin'
With a hundred-dollar bill
Oh when you see me comin'
Heist your window high
Oh when you see me comin'
Heist your window high
Done got bloodthirsty
Don't care how I die
Oh roll me with your stomach
Feed me with your tongue
Roll me with your stomach
Feed me with your tongue
Dirty longtime baby
Till you make me come

Halimuhfask

Hurston: I heard "Halimuhfask" down on the east coast.

Halpert: Who did you hear it from, and when?

Hurston: I don't remember. I was in a big crowd. And I learned it in the evening during the crowd. And I just don't exactly remember who did teach it to me, but I learned it mostly from the crowd.

You may leave and go to Halimuhfask
But my slow drag will bring you back
Oh you may go, but this will bring you back.

Oh been in the country, but I've moved to town
I'm a slooow shaker from a head on down
Oh you may go, but this will bring you back.

Oh some folks call me a solo shaker
What a doggone lie, I am a backbone breaker
Well you may go, but this will bring you back.

Oh you like my features, but you don't like me
Don't you like my features, don't you shake my tree
Oh you may go but this will bring you back.

A hoodoo, a hoodoo, a hoodoo wagon
My heels are poppin' now my toenails crackin'
Well you may go, but this will bring you back.

Halpert: You said you learned it in a crowd. How do you learn most of your songs?

Hurston: I learn. I just get in the crowd with the people if they are singing and I listen as best I can and then I start to join in with a phrase or two and then finally I get so I can sing a verse and then I keep on till I learn all the sounds and all the verses and then I sing them back to the people, until they tell me that I can sing them just like them. And then I take part and try it out on different people, who already know the song, until they are quite satisfied that I know it. Then I carry it in my memory.

Halpert: Well, how about those that you have in your book and publish in the journals?

Hurston: Well, that is the same way I got them. I learned the song myself and then I can take it with me wherever I go. (Break in tape)

Tampa

Hurston: This song is called "Tampa." I have known it ever since I could remember, so I don't know who taught it to me. But I heard it sung in my native village when I was a child. Not in front of the old folks, of course.

Oh thought I heard somebody say
Your nasty butt your stinky butt take it away
Oh your nasty butt your stinky butt take it away
I do not want it in here.

Oh I am so glad that the lawyers pay
The women in Tampa got to watch the air
Oh I do not want it in here.

Oh thought I heard somebody shout
Hoist up the window let the stink go out
Oh hoist up the window let the stink go out
I do not want it in here.

Oh since I heard somebody say
Your nasty butt your stinky butt take it away
Oh your nasty butt your stinky butt take it away
I do not want it in here.

Oh since I heard somebody say . . .

Halpert: You say it was only sung by children?

Hurston: I have known it all my life, though it was not confined to children. Everybody sung and danced on it. And you had Negro orchestras, the local orchestras, often played it, the tune. They didn't sing the words, but the tune is one of the very favorite dance tunes.

Poor Boy or Poor Gal

Hurston: This one, some of them call it "Poor Boy" and some of them call it "Poor Gal," but it's a pretty well distributed blues tune all over the South. The words do not rhyme. It's the typical Negro pattern of the same line repeated three times with a sort of flip line on the end. And the change is in the tune rather than the words for the most part.

Halpert: Where did you pick up the way you sing it?

Hurston: I've known that all my life, but I kept learning verses as I gone around.

Poor gal, long ways from home
Oh poor gal, long ways from home
Poor gal, long ways from home.

Oh lady in jail, my back's down to the wall
Lady in jail, back's down to the wall
Oh lady in jail, my back's down to the wall.

Oh don't you hear that east coast when she blows
Oh don't you hear that east coast when she blows
Oh don't you hear that east coast when she blows.

Come at a time when a woman won't need no man
Oh, comes at a time when a woman won't need no man
Oh, comes at a time when a woman won't need no man.

See you when your troubles get like mine
Oh, see you when your troubles get like mine
I'll see you when your troubles get like mine.

You mistreat me, you mistreat a marvelous gal
Oh, mistreat me, mistreat a marvelous gal
Oh, you mistreat me, you mistreat a marvelous gal.

Oh I'll see you when your troubles get like mine
Oh I'll see you when your troubles get like mine
Oh I'll see you when your troubles get like mine.

Missing me, missing me, are you missing that marvelous gal.

I am way down in Florida on the haul
Oh, way down in Florida on the haul
I am way down in Florida on the haul.

Mama Don't Want No Peas, No Rice

Hurston: "Mama Don't Want No Peas, No Rice" is a song from Nassau of the Bahama Islands. They are great sound makers and their tunes are decidedly more African than the ones made by the Negroes in America. They make songs so rapidly, they say anything you do, we put you in tune, and in a few hours they have a song about it. And "Mama Don't Want No Peas, No Rice" is about a woman that wanted to stay drunk all the time, and her husband is really complaining about it. He is explaining to the neighbors what is the matter with his wife and why they don't get along better.

Mama don't want no peas, no rice
No coconut oil, no coconut oil
Mama don't want no peas, no rice
No coconut oil, no coconut oil
Mama don't want no peas, no rice, no coconut oil
All she wants is whiskey, brandy all the time.

Make up my bed last night over the wall, over the wall
Make up my bed last night over the wall, over the wall
Make up my bed last night over the wall, over the wall
All she wants is whiskey, brandy all the time.

Mama don't feel so very good across the chest
Mama don't feel so very good across the chest
Mama don't feel so very good across the chest
All she wants is whiskey, brandy all the time.

Oh mama she went to bed last night feeling cold, feeling cold
Mama she went to bed last night feeling cold, feeling cold
Mama she went to bed last night feeling cold
All she want is whiskey, brandy all the time.

Oh mama she don't drink no gin because of sin, because of sin
Oh mama don't drink no gin because of sin, because of sin
Oh mama don't drink no gin because of sin
All she wants is whiskey, brandy all the time.

Oh mama she said to papa he's getting old, getting old
Mama she said to papa he's getting old, getting old
Mama she said to papa he's getting old, getting old
All she wants is whiskey, brandy all the time.

So mama don't want no peas, no rice,
No coconut oil, no coconut oil
Mama don't want no peas, no rice,
No coconut oil, no coconut oil
All she wants is whiskey, brandy all the time

The Crow Dance

Hurston: This dance evidently came from Africa. Dr. Herskovits says he saw the background of it in West Africa. The crow in some way seems to be sacred in Africa. But what they are talking about is what we know in the United States as the buzzard. And the buzzard comes to get something to eat and they are talking about it, and they dance it. And one person gets in the center and imitates the buzzard, and the rest of them fall in the background.

Oh ma-ma come see dat crow!
See how he flies!
Oh ma-ma come see dat crow
See how he flies!
Dis crow, dis crow, goin' to fly tonight
See how he flies!
Dis crow, dis crow, goin' to fly tonight
See how he flies!
Oh ma-ma-ma come see dat crow
See how he flies!
Oh ma-ma-ma come see dat crow
Dis crow, dis crow, goin' to fly tonight
See how he flies!
Dis crow, dis crow, goin' to fly tonight
See how he flies!
See how he flies!
Oh ma-ma-ma come see dis crow
See how he flies!
Cawh!

Shack Rouser

Hurston: In all the big work camps, sawmills, and sometimes still in the road camps and whatnot, they have a man that go down and wake up the camp. And he has various chants and hollers to wake them up, and sometimes he makes them up as he goes along.

Halpert: Could you tell us where you heard them?

Hurston: Well, I heard these at the Loughman, a big sawmill down in Polk County.

Wake up bullies!
Get on the ruuunn!
'Tain't quite day but it's five o'clock!

Hurston: The shack rouser then shouts: "Come out under dat cover, bullies, come on out from under that cover, unless you want some trouble with the worker."

Wake up Jacob
Day's a-breakin'
Get your whole cut of bacon
And your shirttail shakin'.

You rowdy muleskinners
You better learn how to skin
Cap'n got a new job
And they need a hundred men.

The Fire Dance

[Note: the interview before this song is conducted by Dr. Carita Doggett Corse rather than Halpert.]

Dr. Corse: What kind of a song is this, Zora?

Hurston: This is a natural song from the Bahamas.

Dr. Corse: When is it used?

Hurston: Well, they sing this song when they are jumping the fire dance.

Dr. Corse: What is the fire dance?

Hurston: The fire dance is some sort of African survival in the West Indies and they beat the drums and sing these little songs.

Dr. Corse: And how did you happen to learn it?

Hurston: Well, I was doing research down there, songs, under Columbia University, and collected quite a few of them. And this is just one of them.

Mr. Brown I want you daughter
Oh Mr. Brown
Court her like a lady
Oh Mr. Brown
Young lady
Oh Mr. Brown
Oh Mr. Brown
Oh Mr. Brown
Oh Mr. Brown
Oh Mr. Brown
Oh Mr. Brown

Young lady
Oh Mr. Brown
Oh Mr. Brown

Hurston: And they keep that up until the drum is cold and then they change it and sing another song of the same kind.

Dr. Corse: A song of the same kind?

Hurston: This little song is a story. The young lady thinks that it is time for them to get married. In fact, she thinks that they just have to, and the boy doesn't want to marry, and so this song is about it.

Willie lend me your pigeon
Keep company with mine
Tillie lend me your pigeon
Keep company with mine.
My pigeon gone wild in the bush
My pigeon gone wild
My pigeon gone wild in the bush
My pigeon gone wild.

Evalina, you know the baby don't favor me, eh
You know the baby don't favor me, eh
Evalina, Evalina, don't tell your mama you belong to me, eh
You know the baby don't favor me.

Dr. Corse: Are those songs sung in Florida as well as the West Indies?

Hurston: Yes, Dr. Corse. They are sung in Key West, and Miami, and Palm Beach, and out in the Everglades, where a great number of Nassaus are working in the bean fields and whatnot. There are a great number of them in Florida. They hold jumping dances every week.

Corse: I think it is very interesting that we have influences from the West Indies as well as from the rural South in Florida Negro folklore.

Notes

Foreword

1. ZNH to Carl Van Vechten, Beineke Collection, Yale. This letter, dated February 1939, spoke of her desire "to bolt the Project" and attend a folklore festival in St. Louis.
2. Toni Cade Bambera, ed., *The Sanctified Church* (Berkeley, Calif.: Turtle Island, 1981).
3. Gary McDonough, ed., *The Florida Negro: A Federal Writer's Project Legacy* (Jackson, Miss.: University Press of Mississippi, 1993).

Part One: Zora Neale Hurston

1. ZNH, *Dust Tracks on a Road* (Philadelphia: J. B. Lippincott, 1942), 1.
2. The Hurston Bible that once belonged to John and Lula Hurston, Zora's parents, is in the possession of their grandaughter and Zora's niece, Winifred Hurston Clark, of Memphis, Tennessee. The location of the Bible and an accompanying interview with Ms. Clark formed the basis of my article "New Tracks on *Dust Tracks:* Toward a Reassessment of the Life of Zora Neale Hurston," *African American Review*, March 1997, 5–21, in which I give a full account of the Bible's location, discuss the important information that it contains, and underscore the discrepancies with Zora Neale Hurston's assertions.
3. Theodore Rosengarten, *All God's Dangers: The Life of Nate Shaw* (New York: Alfred A. Knopf, 1975), 299. Shaw's narrative poignantly details the poverty and deprivation of the Alabama hinterland that the Hurstons left behind.
4. Hurston's vivid description of Notasulga in her first novel, *Jonah's Gourd Vine*, leads one to believe that she must have visited it

frequently during her growing-up years. In *Dust Tracks* she speaks of her mother traveling back to Alabama to tend her sick mother. On trips like these, she must have brought young Zora with her. Thus the young Zora saw firsthand how her relatives the Pottses lived, a life that contrasted sharply with the promise and prosperity of the Florida scene. As a deeply perceptive child, she came to know the difference between poverty and plenty, between racial and economic degradation and self-sufficiency and freedom.

5. ZNH, *Jonah's Gourd Vine* (Philadelphia: Lippincott, 1934), 107.

6. ZNH, *Dust Tracks*, 5.

7. See Bordelon, "New Tracks," 8–9, for a full discussion of the year of their migration. Her father's migration before her birth explains why he did not attend it.

8. R. Otey, *Eatonville, Florida: A Brief History of One of America's First Freemen's Towns* (Winter Park: Four G Publishers, 1989), 16–17.

9. Ibid.

10. ZNH, *Dust Tracks*, 13.

11. The marriage took place on February 14, 1905. Marriage Licenses, Orange County Records, 262.

12. ZNH, *Dust Tracks*, 75.

13. The fullest account of Hurston's feelings is found in *Dust Tracks*. She skips exact details of her whereabouts.

14. *Thirteenth Census of the United States: Population* (Washington, D.C.: Government Printing Office, 1912), 112.

15. ZNH, *Dust Tracks*, 124–25.

16. Church Register, Bethel Baptist Church, Jacksonville, 1914. Telephone interview with Camilla Thompson, December 1997.

17. Hurston, *Dust Tracks*, 93–94.

18. Margaret Walker, *Richard Wright: Daemonic Genius* (New York: Warner, 1988), 40–50.

19. Interview with Winifred Hurston Clark.

20. ZNH, *Dust Tracks*, 94.

21. Interview with Winifred Hurston Clark.

22. *Dust Tracks* leads the reader to believe that following her flight from her brother's home, Hurston did not see Bob for at least a decade. Hurston wrote: "While in the field, I drove to Memphis and had a beautiful reconciliation with Bob, my oldest brother, and his family. We had not seen each other since I ran off to be a lady's maid." The first of these visits probably occurred during the summer of 1927 when Hurston was doing summer fieldwork while attending Barnard College. Following this initial visit, Hurston made others, becoming

a well-known figure in the Scott Street neighborhood community. ZNH, *Dust Tracks*, 94–98; interview with Zora Mack (Sarah Hurston's daughter), January 26, 1994, Eatonville, Fla.

23. ZNH, *Dust Tracks*, 105–13; Robert E. Hemenway, *Zora Neale Hurston: A Literary Biography* (Urbana: University of Illinois Press, 1977), 18; interview with Zora Mack.
24. Hemenway, *ZNH*, 35–59: Hurston, *Dust Tracks*, 113–22.
25. ZNH, *Dust Tracks*, 122–25.
26. Hemenway, *ZNH*, 60–65.
27. The best record of these field trips is found in Hurston's correspondence with Mrs. Mason. These letters are among the Alain Locke Papers, Moorland-Spingarn Research Center, Howard University, Washington, D.C.
28. ZNH, *Dust Tracks*, 129–39.
29. Ibid., 153.
30. Ibid., 127–56.
31. H. Kamau, "Interview with Dr. Margaret Walker Alexander," 1986, Amistad Research Center, Tulane University, New Orleans.
32. Hemenway, *ZNH*, 153–56.
33. For an insightful view of the Federal Writers' Project, see Jerre Mangione, *The Dream and the Deal* (Boston: Little, Brown, 1973).
34. ZNH, "Hoodoo in America," *Journal of American Folklore* 44:392; ZNH, *Mules and Men*, 183–246.
35. See the chapter "Congress Sees Red" in Mangione, *Dream and the Deal*, for a running account of the conservatives' reaction to the WPA projects.
36. Federal Writers' Project, Virginia, *The Negro in Virginia* (New York: Hastings House, 1940).
37. Florida File, Office of Negro Affairs, Central Files, FWP, RG 69, National Archives (hereafter cited as NA).
38. Mangione, *Dream and the Deal*, 210–11, 258–63; Hemenway, *ZNH*, 248, 251; McConkey to Alsberg, April 22, 1938, Field Reports, Florida, FWP, RG 69, NA.
39. Alsberg to Katherine Kellock, Jan. 22, 1936, Field Reports, FWP, RG 69, NA. See also Pamela G. Bordelon, "Mirror to America: The Federal Writers' Project's Florida Reflection," Ph.D. Diss., Louisiana State University, 1991.
40. Hurston's enrollment on a security wage basis is confirmed in Darel McConkey to Alsberg, April 22, 1938, Field Reports, Florida, FWP, RG 69, NA; and by author's interview with Stetson Kennedy, Aug. 6, 1988. See also *Final Report on the WPA Program* (Washington, D.C.: Government Printing Office, 1946), 18–20.

41. Mangione, *Dream and the Deal*, 53–56; Monty Noam Penkower, *The Federal Writers' Project: A Study in Government Patronage and the Arts* (Urbana: University of Illinois Press, 1971), 67, 18–20; William F. McDonald, *Federal Relief Administration and the Arts* (Columbus: Ohio State University, 1969), 663–65.

42. Interview with Stetson Kennedy, Aug. 6, 1988.

43. Early manuscripts bore the titles "The History of the Negro in Florida" (1936) and "The Negro in Florida" (1940). Both of these manuscripts are found in the Special Collections Department, P. K. Yonge Library, University of Florida, Gainesville (hereafter cited as PKYL).

44. Alsberg to Corse, June 21, 1938, Central Correspondence, Florida, FWP, RG 69, NA.

45. See Sterling Brown correspondence, Florida File, Office of Negro Affairs, Central Files, FWP, RG 69, NA, for the best account of his battle. Edward Rodrigues to Alsberg, Oct. 7, 1935, Administrative Correspondence, Florida, FWP, RG 69, NA. This insightful letter details the shutting out of blacks from the arts projects in Florida. Interview with Stetson Kennedy, Aug. 6, 1988.

46. Bordelon, "Mirror to America," 31–62, discusses the state's FWP administrative setup. The central files are filled with correspondence regarding hiring, salaries, political appointments, and the like. Carita Corse made $191 per month. See Central Files, Florida, FWP, RG 69, NA.

47. This incident demonstrates the hidden powers that state WPA organizations exercised over the arts projects. When the arts program began, the New Deal purposely created dual lines of administration that gave state WPA organizations control over employment and finances. National offices of the programs had control only over technical matters. Although this was initially seen as a cost-cutting administrative measure, the New Deal in effect created a huge pork barrel for state politicians and congressmen, whose support it deemed vital for the ultimate success of their social programs.

48. ZNH to Christopher Publishing House, May 5, 1939, Hurston File, Florida Negro Collection, Florida Historical Society Library, Cocoa Beach, Florida (hereafter cited as FNC).

49. Corse's publications included *Florida, Empire of the Sun* (Tallahassee: State Hotel Commission, 1930); and *Dr. Andrew Turnbull and the New Smyrna Colony of Florida* (Chapel Hill: University of North Carolina Press, 1919).

50. Interviews with Stetson Kennedy, Aug. 2, 1988, and Jan. 6, 1989; Jacob Baker to C. B. Treadway, Oct. 5, 1935, Cronyn to Treadway, Oct. 7,

1935, Cronyn Files, Administrative Correspondence, Florida, FWP, RG 69, NA; Nancy Williams, "Interview with Dr. Carita Doggett Corse, the State Director of the Writers' Project in Florida," New Smyrna Beach, Fla., March 18, 1976, PKYL; *Final Report on the WPA Program*, 4; Penkower, *Federal Writers' Project*, 38–41; "Corse File," Files of Henry G. Alsberg, FWP, RG 69, NA; Alsberg to Bernice Babcock, Jan. 13, 1936, "State Directors Who's Who" file, Federal Writers' Project Papers, Historic New Orleans Collection, New Orleans, La. (hereafter cited as HNC).

51. Corse graduated from Vassar College in 1913 and was awarded a master's degree from Columbia in 1916. In recognition of her work in early Spanish history and her contribution to literature, the University of the South awarded her an honorary doctorate in 1932. From that time on Corse added the title to her name, and in FWP circles her nickname became "Doctor."

52. Corse to Alsberg, June 21, 1938, Florida File, Files of HGA, FWP, RG 69, NA; Williams, "Interview with Dr. Carita Doggett Corse."

53. ZNH, "The 'Pet' Negro System," in Alice Walker, ed., *I Love Myself When I Am Laughing* (New York: Feminist Press, 1979), 157.

54. ZNH to Corse, Dec. 3, 1938, Hurston Collection, Special Collections, PKYL.

55. Corse to Alsberg, June 14, 1938, FWP, Florida, RG 69, NA.

56. Interview with Stetson Kennedy, Aug. 6, 1988.

57. John Corse, the younger of Corse's two sons, vividly remembers meeting Hurston in his home as a young boy. Telephone interview with John Corse, May 1993.

58. Williams, "Interview with Dr. Carita Doggett Corse."

59. ZNH to Corse, Dec. 3, 1938, Hurston Collection, Special Collections, PKYL.

60. Interview with Winifred Hurston Clark. See also Bordelon, "New Tracks on *Dust Tracks.*"

61. Interview with Winifred Hurston Clark.

62. John Calvin Hamilton and Wilhelmina Hurston, Marriage License, Aug. 15, 1938, Orange County Records, No. 10, 314.

63. Interview with Winifred Hurston Clark.

64. Paul Diggs, "House by the Lake," September 1938, FNC.

65. Interview with Winifred Hurston Clark.

66. ZNH, *Dust Tracks*, 128.

67. See ibid., 127–49, chapter titled "Research," for Hurston's explanation of her fieldwork.

68. See *Tell My Horse*, 229–64. Wade Davis, *The Serpent and the*

Rainbow (New York: Warner Books, 1985), discusses the secret societies that for generations guarded the secret of the zombies. Hurston was the first anthropologist to examine one of their victims who had been zombified. She photographed the woman and concluded, after discussion with the attending physician, that the state was, as Davis puts it, "not a case of awakening the dead, but a matter of a semblance of death induced by some drug known to a few." This key discovery, totally ignored by Hurston's colleagues at the time, years later led Wade Davis on his odyssey.

69. For a discussion of Botkin's career and views on folklore see Jerrold Hirsch, "Folklore in the Making: B. A. Botkin," *Journal of American Folklore*, Jan.–Mar. 1987, 3–38. Botkin's own writings include "We Called it Living Lore," *New York Folklore Quarterly* 14 (Autumn 1958): 189–201; and "WPA and Folklore Research: 'Bread and Song,' " *Southern Folklore Quarterly* 1 (March 1939): 10.

70. FWP, *Manual for Folklore Studies*, Folklore Files, FWP, RG 69, NA.

71. Kellock to Alsberg, Jan. 22, 1936, Field Reports, and 69, Corse to Kellock, Jan. 31, 1936, Administrative Correspondence, Florida, WPA, RG 69, NA. For all practical purposes, the city descriptions, listed in a separate section for ready reference, were part of the auto tours.

72. Charles Ward to Gordon Adams, Aug. 13, 1936, FWP Collection, FHS, Melbourne, Fla.

73. The entire story is contained in Field Reports, Florida, FWP, RG 69, NA, and in Bordelon, "Mirror to America," 153–85.

74. "Instructions: Folklore and Folk Customs," 8551, FWP, RG 69, NA; see also "Correspondence Pertaining to Folklore Studies, 1936–1941," FL, FWP, RG 69, NA.

75. "Instructions: Folklore and Folk Customs."

76. Michael E. Staub, *Voices of Persuasion: Politics of Representation in 1930s America* (New York: Cambridge Press, 1994), 81. In this provocative study, Staub looks at much of the "reality-based writings of the Depression era." He applies this thesis to Hurston's *Mules and Men*, but her FWP folklore proves just as valid a source for this interpretation.

77. See Harvard Sitkoff, *A New Deal for Blacks* (New York: Oxford University Press, 1977) 34–57. Sitkoff traces the explicit political reasons, such as the swing vote in a number of Northern cities, and the other factors that led to New Deal awareness of and assistance for African Americans.

78. During the fall months of 1935, when the WPA arts projects were launched in the states, racial inequities immediately revealed

themselves. Highly qualified African Americans applied in Florida only to be told that it was too late to receive the aid. Knowing that few of the positions had been filled, disgruntled white-collar blacks wrote black leaders in Washington, men like John P. Davis, director of the National Negro Congress, who served as a vigilant watchdog for African American concerns, and Walter White, a special friend of Eleanor Roosevelt. These unsuccessful job seekers related countless stories of racial slight. Black intellectuals were given picks and shovels and assigned to construction projects. In January 1936, an FWP field representative visiting Florida reported seeing black Ph.D.s "doing ditch-digging or little better." In late November 1935, Alsberg attended a banquet at Howard University with a number of black leaders to discuss the organization of a national unit of black writers to research the nation's African American roots. These early plans were later scratched in favor of city and state units. New York and Chicago hired black writers, including aspiring novices like Richard Wright and Ralph Ellison. Louisiana, Florida, and Virginia, states with more liberal FWP directors, implemented their own "Negro Units."

79. Cronyn to Baker, "Negro Cultural Project of American Guide," November 30, 1935, Files of George Cronyn, FWP, RG 69, NA; Mangione, *Dream and the Deal*, 210–11, 258–59, 262–63; Penkower, *Federal Writers Project*, 140–47. "The Portrait of the Negro as an American" never moved beyond the planning stages. Brown did write the chapter chronicling African American history for *Washington: City and Capital* (1937). His frank treatment of miscegenation and criticism of slavery conducted in the shadows of the Capitol itself angered a number of Southern congressmen.

80. Other Southern states were unable to garner the local and state support needed to implement and sustain these units. FWP directors offered excuses. For example, the Alabama director claimed that suitable blacks could not be found, despite the presence of institutions of higher learning like Tuskeegee.

81. The unit was housed with other black arts and WPA recreational projects at the Clara White Mission in the black section of Jacksonville. Alsberg to Corse, Feb. 20, 1936, and Corse to Alsberg, Mar. 5, 1936, Administrative Files, Florida, FWP, RG 69, NA, details the establishment of the unit. The names of the members of the Florida Negro Unit are never mentioned in official correspondence, but can be derived from the raw manuscripts that they produced during their first year. There is very little official correspondence discussing their activities. Sources include Gary R. Mormino, "Florida Slave Narratives,"

Florida Historical Quarterly, April 1988, 399–419; and, interviews with Stetson Kennedy, Aug. 2, 1988, and Jan. 6, 1989.

82. Dozens of former bondsmen, many of whom were still living in the areas of their enslavement, spoke willingly with their black interviewers. Their testimony produced stunning, candid information. See Mormino, "Florida Slave Narratives."

83. FWP, Florida, "The History of the Negro in Florida," manuscript, PKYL.

84. Walker, *Richard Wright*. See the chapter "The WPA 'Stairway to the Stars,' " 68–85, for an account of Wright's WPA years. Walker discusses the *Story* contest as well, 116–19.

85. Sterling Brown's review is reprinted, along with other reviews, in Henry Louis Gates, Jr., and K. A. Appiah, *Zora Neale Hurston: Critical Perspectives Past and Present* (New York: Amistad Press, 1993), 20–21.

86. "Art and Such," Florida Negro Files, FHL, Tampa; Sterling Brown correspondence, Office of Negro Affairs, Central Files, FWP, RG 69, NA.

87. Richard Wright, "Their Eyes Were Watching God," in Gates and Appiah, eds., *ZNH: Critical Perspectives*, 16–17. The review appeared in *New Masses*, Oct. 5, 1937.

88. Viola Muse, "Sanctified Church," July 30, 1936, FNC, 57–64.

89. FWP, Florida, "Negro Churches," PKYL.

90. ZNH to Langston Hughes, Dec. 1929, Beinecke Collection, Yale.

91. ZNH, "Ritualistic Expression from the lips of the Communicants of the Seventh Day Church of God, Beaufort, South Carolina," Margaret Mead Papers, Container 5, Manuscript Division, Library of Congress.

92. Eric J. Sunquist, "The Drum with a Man Skin," in Gates and Appiah, eds., *ZNH: Critical Perspectives*, 39–66.

93. Interview with Abbot Ferris, December 1994, Washington, D.C. I met Dr. Ferris at the Library of Congress Symposium "American Stuff," in which he shared his participation in the field recordings. Like many other federal writers, Ferris went on to a distinguished career in folklore. See Abbott L. Ferris, "Rabbit Singing Games of Mississippi Children," *Mississippi Folklore Register* 24 (1990), 3–16.

94. ZNH, "New Children's Games," FNC.

95. Typescripts of them cite later dates, but this reflects the FWP's practice of dating a piece by its typing rather than actual writing date.

96. Christopher Publishing House to ZNH, May 10, 1939, FNC; Macmillan Company to ZNH, FNC. Macmillan turned the manuscript down flat, writing, "There is no place where such a volume would fit in with our publishing schedule."

97. See Walter Goodman, *The Committee: The Extraordinary Career of the House Committee on Un-American Activies* (New York: Farrar, Straus & Giroux, 1964). Unsubstantiated charges were leveled that known Communists worked on the Federal Writers' and Theater Projects. WPA rules strictly forbade political activity on its projects, and the workers involved were dismissed.

98. "National Exhibition of Skills," pamphlet, in Information Division Files, Florida, FWP, RG 69, NA. This WPA information bulletin registers the types of publicity-related activities that the WPA conducted in order to get its work before the public.

99. Hemenway, *ZNH*, 178–84.

100. Interview with Winifred Hurston Clark.

101. "From Sun to Sun," Hurston Files, FNC.

102. ZNH, "Dance Songs and Tales from the Bahamas," *Journal of American Folklore* 43 (July–Sept. 1930), 294–312.

103. Interview with Carita Doggett Corse.

104. McDonald, *Federal Relief*, 720; Botkin, "Bread and Song," 11.

105. John A. Lomax to Corse, April 3, 1937, Folklore File, Florida, Central Files, FWP, RG 69, NA.

106. This folklore can be found in WPA files, Florida Bureau of Folklife, Department of State, Tallahassee, Fla.

107. Botkin to Corse, May 26, 1939, Folklore File, Florida, Central Files, FWP, RG 69, NA.

108. Hurston's trip to Cross City has been reconstructed through the writers' reports: ZNH, "Turpentine Camp—Cross City," PKYL; Robert Cook, "Photographing the Turpentine Industry at Cross City, Florida," PKYL; William Duncan, "Report on Trip to Cross City," PKYL.

109. Interview with Clifford Clark.

110. Duncan, "Report on Trip to Cross City."

111. ZNH, "Turpentine Camp—Cross City."

112. The original manuscript, "Turpentine," is published for the first time in this collection.

113. ZNH, *Seraph on the Suwannee* (New York: Scribner's, 1948), 42.

114. ZNH, "Turpentine Camp—Cross City."

115. Hemenway, *ZNH*, 111–33.

116. ZNH, "Turpentine Camp—Cross City."

117. Ibid.

118. Michael D'Orso, *Like Judgment Day: The Ruin and Redemption of a Town Called Rosewood* (New York: Berkeley, 1996); interview with Clifford Clark.

119. ZNH, "Turpentine Camp—Cross City."

120. Duncan, "Report on Trip to Cross City," 3.
121. ZNH, "Turpentine Camp—Cross City"; Lawrence Levine, *Black Culture and Black Consciousness* (New York: Oxford, 1977), 344–58.
122. Interview with Clifford Clark.
123. Herbert Halpert, "Coming into Folklore More Than Fifty Years Ago," *Journal of American Folklore* 105 (Fall 1992), 442.
124. Record 2, AI, A2, Aug. 16, 1939, WPA Recordings, Florida Bureau of Folklife, Tallahassee; Stetston Kennedy, "The Federal Writers' Project I Knew," "In the Nick of Time: A Symposium on Folklore Collection by the WPA Florida Writers' Project," Feb. 4, 1989.
125. Record 2, AI, A2.
126. Hemenway, *ZNH*, 253.
127. Mangione, *Dream and the Deal*, 329–48: McDonald, *Federal Relief*, 305–40.
128. Hemenway, *ZNH*, 273–75.
129. Judging from the Florida collection, only a fraction of what must have been thousands of cubic feet of state records ended up in the Library of Congress and the National Archives. The bulk of the Florida FWP files remained in the state. Some of Hurston's writings were forwarded to Botkin in Washington and were deposited either in the manuscript division or the Folklife Center. Most of her writings, however, remained with the black writers' field copy. Most of this documentation was given to the Florida Historical Society Library.

Record disbursement took place during the darkest days of World War II, and few believed the field copy collected by writers on relief had any value. A librarian at the University of Florida (now retired) once remarked, "What did they know? They were on relief." Florida FWP director Corse sent trainloads of project materials to the University of Florida, sponsor of the FWP in 1940–41, only to learn some time later that librarians had sorted through the files, kept some of the materials, and thrown away the remainder. Of the three hundred photographs made at Cross City, only those appearing in this volume were saved, including Hurston's portrait sitting on a turpentiner's porch. Corse explained in an interview years later, "The attitude they had was that it was a defunct project."

Part Two: Readings

1. Martin Richardson, "John Henry, 1937 Model," Folklore and Custom, FNC.
2. Toni Cade Bambara, ed., *The Sanctified Church* (Berkeley, Calif.: Turtle Island, 1981), 41–48. When compiling *The Sanctified Church*,

Ms. Bambara included Richardson's folk tales and mistakenly cited them as Hurston's. In addition, the selections "Father Abraham" and "Cures and Beliefs" are not Hurston's work, but tales collected by other field writers.

3. ZNH, "Spirituals and Neo-Spirituals," in Nancy Cunard, ed., *Negro: An Anthology* (London: Wishert, 1934), 359–61.

4. Only recently have scholars spoken of such things as "cultural borrowings" and links to the African past, as Hurston discussed years earlier in this essay. See Eric Sunquist, "Drum with a Man Skin," in Henry Louis Gates, Jr., and K. A. Appiah, *Zora Neale Hurston: Critical Perspectives Past and Present* (New York: Amistad Press, 1993), 39–66. In this essay Sunquist explores these continuities and points out Hurston's brilliant recall of them. He asserts that Hurston viewed African retention in folk religion "as a powerful, formative undercurrent or syncretism that had been thoroughly absorbed in Afro Christian practice" and notes that in his ability to call forth the congregation, the preacher was "a drum with a man skin" (p. 50). See also Eric Lincoln and Lawrence H. Mamiya, *The Black Church in the African American Experience* (Durham, N.C.: Duke University Press, 1990), 17. The authors make no mention of Hurston's early contributions, however, and draw no parallels between their findings and hers. See their chapter "Music and the Black Church."

5. Pete Daniel, *The Shadow of Slavery: Peonage in the South, 1901–1969* (Urbana: University of Illinois Press, 1972), provides one of the best accounts of peonage and the turpentine industry in Florida.

6. FWP, *Florida*, 431. National folklore editor Benjamin Botkin took such delight in the tale that he reprinted "Diddy-Wah-Diddy" in *A Treasury of Southern Folklore* (New York: Crown, 1949), 479–80.

7. Hurston's version of "Heaven" corresponds with "A Flying Fool" in Abrahams's *Afro-American Folktales*. In this slightly different account, a black man denied entrance into "white man's heaven" by St. Peter slipped in anyway, stole a pair of wings, and really went flying, "having himself a good ol' time." The heavenly police eventually caught up with him and threw him out. But as he told his friend later, "Yeah, they may not let any colored folks in, but while I was there I was a heavenly fool." See Roger Abrahams, ed., *Afro-American Folktales: Stories from Black Traditions in the New World* (New York: Pantheon, 1985), 280–81, 265.

8. See ZNH, "High John de Conquer," in Dundes, ed., *Mother Wit from the Laughing Barrel* (Jackson, Miss.: University Presses of Mississippi, 1990), 542–44.

9. ZNH, *Their Eyes Were Watching God*, 192–93.
10. FWP, *Florida*, 474.
11. Ibid., 366; ZNH, *Mules and Men*, 118–19.
12. FWP, *Florida*, 362.
13. Interview with Stetson Kennedy, Aug. 6, 1988.
14. ZNH, *Mules and Men*, 1.
15. Writers followed guidelines in FWP, "Instructions: Folklore and Folk Customs," 8551, Bound Copies of Instructions, The American Guide, FWP, RG 69, NA. These first instructions, written by Katherine Kellock, reflect Henry Alsberg's basic ideas about the guide project and folklore.
16. Every tour contained dozens of thumbnail sketches of the towns along the route. The goal was to produce information that had never been published. By consulting old newspaper files and courthouse records and, most important of all, interviewing old residents who knew the area's history better than anyone else, the FWP achieved its goal. Hurston's background research drew from these sources as well.
17. Corse to Harry L. Shaw, Jr., June 22, 1938, Lexicon of Trade Jargon Folder, Florida Files, FWP, RG 69, NA.
18. FWP, *Florida*, 475.
19. The excerpt is found in FWP, *Florida*, 457. As was the case with "The Ocoee Riot," the inclusion of this passage in the state book marked a triumph for the editorial camp known as "realists," who wanted to illuminate the state's contemporary life "warts and all." If the book had received its final edit in Florida, the strong opposition of Carita Corse and the "moonlight and magnolia" editorial camp would have blocked its inclusion. The literary quality of the passage, its insightful characterization of what life was really like for the migrant, and its focus on the lower economic one-third of the nation dove-tailed perfectly with national FWP goals. For all these reasons Hurston's revealing passage found its way into the Florida guidebook.
20. FWP, *Florida*, 362.
21. The first volume of the Southern interviews had just been published in March 1939 as *These Are Our Lives*. William T. Couch, the project's innovator and director, had plans for several more volumes. Life histories of turpentiners were avidly sought.
22. ZNH, "Citrus Industry," Administrative Correspondence, Florida, Central Files, FWP, RG 69, NA. This Hurston-written field copy, identified by the subject and her terminology, was discovered by accident while sifting through the state's material in the National Archives.

23. Veronica Huss, "We Is Victims," Florida Life Histories, Files. Southern Historical Collection, Chapel Hill, N.C.
24. FWP, *Florida*, 457; ZNH, "The Ocoee Riot," FNC.
25. Tapping her skills as a published writer and long-time Florida resident, Hurston was summoned to the national office in late November 1938, to assist with the final editing of the state book. Protected by Washington's more liberal viewpoint, the black version of the Ocoee riot story was included. If the book had been edited in Florida, Hurston's addition to the state guidebook would most likely have been deleted.
26. Robert E. Hemenway, *Zora Neale Hurston: A Literary Biography* (Urbana: University of Illinois Press, 1977), 174–82.
27. See Maurice O'Sullivan and Jack C. Lane, "Zora Neale Hurston at Rollins College," in Steve Glassman and Kathryn Lee Seidel, eds., *Zora in Florida* (University of Central Florida Press, 1991), 130–45.

Index

Page numbers in *italics* refer to illustrations.

Houseman, John, 13
Howard University, 10, 146
"How the Florida Land Turtle
    Got Its Name" (Hurston),
    xiii, 113
Hughes, Langston, 10–11
Hunter, Max, 27–28
Hurst, Fannie, 10, 17, 143
Hurston, Ben (brother), 6
Hurston, Blanche (sister-in-
    law), 8
Hurston, Everett (brother), 6
Hurston, Isaac (brother), 4
Hurston, Joel (brother), 4, 6
Hurston, John (father), 3, 4, 5, 6,
    7, 48
Hurston, John Cornelius
    (brother), 4, 6, 8, 23
Hurston, Lula "Lucy" Potts
    (mother), 3, 4, 6, 7
Hurston, Mattie Moge (step-
    mother), 6–7
Hurston, Richard (brother), 4
Hurston, Robert, Jr. (nephew),
    8
Hurston, Robert Hezekiah
    (brother), 4, 5–6, 7–9, 21
Hurston, Sarah (sister), 4, 9
Hurston, Wilhelmina (niece),
    see Hamilton, Wilhelmina
    Hurston
Hurston, Wilhelmina (sister-in-
    law), 7–8
Hurston, Winifred, see Clark,
    Winifred Hurston
Hurston, Zora Neale, 50, 54
    autobiographical dissembling
    by, xi, 3–4, 5, 6, 8, 157
    autobiography of, see Dust
    Tracks on a Road
    biographical essay on, xi,
    1–56
    biographical writings on, xi
    birth of, 3
    black writers' criticisms of,
    31–32, 35, 147

childhood of, 4–7
early writing of, 10
earnings of, x, 12, 14, 15, 16
education of, 7, 9–10, 11, 12,
    17
erratic work habits of, xi,
    20–21
as folklorist and
    anthropologist, xi, 10, 11,
    13, 17, 19, 24, 26, 33, 36–37,
    38–39, 46, 60, 68, 89, 158
"missing years" of, 7–9
novels of, see Jonah's Gourd
    Vine; Moses: Man of the
    Mountain; Seraph on the
    Suwanee; Their Eyes Were
    Watching God
pistol carried by, 11, 22
scholarships and grants
    awarded to, 12, 13, 14
second marriage of, x
unpredictability of, 21, 23
writing habits of, 22–23
Hurston family Bible, 3, 5

"Jack and the Beanstalk"
    (Hurston), xiii, 112–13
Jacksonville, Fla., x, xiii, 7, 17,
    20, 23, 29, 30, 33, 45–46, 63,
    64, 143
"Jacksonville Recordings, The"
    (Hurston), xiii, 152, 157–77
Jamaica, 13, 24
J. B. Lippincott, 12
Jenkins, Richard, 65
"John Henry," 73–74, 82–83
Johnson, Charles S., 10
Johnson, Hall, 11
Johnson, James Weldon, 143–44
Johnson, J. M., xii, 29, 33
Johnson, J. Rosamond, 143
John the trickster, 68, 69
Jonah's Gourd Vine (Hurston),
    5, 12, 33, 94, 144
Jones, Orrie, 67
jook joints, 42–43